Getting on with it

What is it?
Ask an older woman

**GLENDA
GARTRELL**

First published by Busybird Publishing 2024

Copyright © 2024 Glenda Gartrell

ISBN:
Paperback: 978-1-923216-59-4
Ebook: 978-1-923216-60-0

Cover design: Busybird Publishing

Layout and typesetting: Busybird Publishing

Busybird Publishing
2/118 Para Road
Montmorency, Victoria
Australia 3094
www.busybird.com.au

The lived experience of those who have typical lives

Contents

Foreword

I was one of the lucky ones. I grew up in regional NSW at the time before the terms adolescent or teenager had been coined. My adult years were spent with trailblazers of the women's movement, with the introduction of the contraceptive pill, the opening of the gates for women to study at university, and the arrival of the world wide web (and social media and internet dating that followed).

My 60-year marriage was a strong, loving partnership. But, *when my husband died when I was 79, I knew no other way to live in the community*. I entered another life stage which is new for me and my generation, completely different from what went before. The notions of intimacy and sexuality for invisible women in their 80s has been taboo. Until now.

I entered this new realm on my own. *I began to wonder how other women were coping. So, I broached the topic with a few other women and from that I learnt about how many older women live.* Together we came to understand that this is the new frontier.

I wrote this conversation starter so that I could share with others – my age and younger – what life was like for the women's movement, my experiences and also, what's been a secret life for most of us. That is, our need of another, one who is not necessarily another half. It's about acknowledging our ongoing social and sexual needs in the later years of our lives.

I don't have to look in the mirror or check the calendar to know I'm in the older woman category – 70s and above. But I'm still the same person with the same personality. Only the lived experience needs an update. I continue to hope that the recognition and respect we afford to gender diverse people, especially the young, might be extended to include the hopes and aspirations of older women.

Preamble

There was a moment when everything changed. Death was in front of me. I knew it was coming but I hadn't anticipated it. And it wasn't his last breath, which was peaceable and without struggle. No, it was immediately after, when I realised I was alone. Really alone. Alone in the house we'd shared for almost half a century; alone in my bed; alone with my thoughts. I'd not anticipated it and now it was an awful reality. My friend Margot had a similar dramatic moment she'd not anticipated, when her spouse surprised her by announcing he was leaving. And he did, then and there. He could not articulate his unhappiness with her undertaking higher education. *I totally missed all the cues about how unhappy he was until one day he came home from work and said he was leaving.* How did we come to understand the change in our lives is here to stay? How did we come to accept both the finality and our new reality? Neither of us think we're atypical, but how can we know that?

A few of us thought the logical place to look for company was online. Only Annette knew what the rest of us discovered through trial and error. Even today, her experience with online relationships makes her seem quite worldly. She'd seen it all before, and she had good advice to share: *Don't give up your girlfriends or your vibrators.* My small sample group had a range of experiences, from Ava's heartbreak to Sophie's lucky escape, and the happy ending for Marion. The experiences of others helps us to understand the differences between socialising with people you've known a while versus getting to know someone online. And then there's the way dating apps work. None of us knew there was a government website with all the advice we needed. If only we'd known before we ventured into the unknown world online. We do now and I've shared this information.

What then, are we all seeking? It continues to be no surprise to us that our need for the touch we share with a special other, does not diminish with age. If anything, it is even more important to our sense of ourselves as well as our pleasure. And we are backed by research which confirms the health benefits of touch and intimacy. Significantly, the need for an intimate other, for someone whose touch is magic, is lifelong. And it's this secret which I explore through my own, and my friends' experiences, and simply wonder why it has remained a secret. How were we persuaded that we are the only ones who want a loving other and, how did we find out that this need has no age limit? Yes, including in aged care, as an experienced sex worker told me.

It didn't take long for a conversation starter with friends for them to share their stories with me. I explore their experiences and my own steep learning curve when I no longer had the comforting touch and intimacy of a loving other half. I accepted my shared life was over, a life that had fulfilled me for six decades. And it's the knowledge from sharing that will help others, before, during and after, they too find themselves alone.

Hopefully, this may prompt researchers to focus on the lived experience typical of older women, how they feel about life and, not just where they live.

Chapter 1

Home alone

…to not feel guilty about wanting to be held

Brigit's story

Brigit

Alone at home after the death of your partner. It's confronting to think about it and it's very confronting when it happens. I was only 43 when my husband died very suddenly in an accident, leaving me with small children to raise alone.

So how did I cope then? Slowly, over some years, I came to realise that there's a difference between being alone, and the deep loneliness stemming from the lack of intimacy. Everybody will have different coping strategies for not being alone… putting the radio on to fill the deafening stillness of an empty house, phoning friends, creating a new routine of life and melding an old one into it. Others remember you are on your own for a while but then they expect you to manage your own life again… by yourself.

Coping with that deep loneliness and lack of intimacy is another matter and I would say it's very individual. It takes time to be able to emotionally accept that your former relationship is physically over and can never return. It takes time to not feel guilty about wanting to be held. It takes time to understand that the heart has many rooms and that your partner will always be in his no matter how many other doors you open.

I had a few fun but not lasting relationships. It took courage to allow myself to be held and to be sexual again, and the relationships wouldn't have started if I had not felt more confident of myself as a separate person. The age of internet dating had not begun.

Only I can seek out people and draw them closer to me if I want company and that to soften that other deep and natural longing for close intimacy with another partner I first have to be OK being my own good.

Margot

After I read *The Feminine Mystique* by Betty Friedan, I joined a group of women seeking to further their education. Alas, it was the beginning of the end of my marriage. I totally missed all the cues about how unhappy he was until one day he came home from work and said he was leaving. We did try marriage guidance counselling, but his heart wasn't in it – he left, and the next day moved in with a woman with whom he was working. Our children were 9 and 7, and I was devastated and on the brink of giving up university, but the other women – all mature-aged students – convinced me to keep studying.

I'd had a satisfying and enjoyable sex life in marriage, and I felt bereft and completely rejected. I did note that the marriage break-up rate of mature-age women students at Macquarie University was running at about 50%. I knew I was not alone in coordinating shared parenting and study. With a few of the women I'd met, we visited bars and various dating sites.

I was keen to try these new venues but was disappointed. In the workforce after graduation, I attracted the attention of a lot of married men. I wasn't flirting with them, but they must have seen my longing for intimacy. I'm not proud of these liaisons, which I always saw as convenient for both parties. They were intelligent men; I had evenings out, good conversations and sex which satisfied us both. It was part of life working for Canberra MPs. But it seemed almost impossible for me to meet single men with whom I had a rapport and shared philosophies. Eventually, my self-esteem improved as I became more successful in my jobs; after menopause, the urge for sex didn't seem so strong. Then again, I always had a vibrator.

***

As his lifeless body was carried out of the house we'd shared for almost 50 years - he'd donated his body to a medical school for student education – I was in a state of shock. Grief, of course, but tempered by the comforting knowledge that he was ready for his death: but, despite everything in front of me, I was not. He'd anticipated the moment and mentioned it to the caring home nursing team a day or two previously. I didn't – or couldn't. Nothing prepares us for our new role in life alone, without our long term other. Yes, for many of us, our other half. I wondered what was going to happen to me now. There's no age when it seems natural for our other half to die. Whether it's sudden, like it was for Brigit, in her forties, or for me at 79, we both felt the haunting aloneness that came with our dramatically altered lives. It was more than altering; it was shattering normality we both expected to go on, and so neither of us was ready.

But it's not the shock, the loss, the grief that comes with the death of a loved one, but what happens next that concerns us here. There were over 30 years between Brigit's and my ages, but the similarities in how our lives unfolded as we coped with our new status, are striking. We didn't know each other well until some years after we both became widows – a title neither of us is comfortable using. Understandably, no one knows how they will feel when a loved one dies, but we're wondering why there is so little discussion of how women of any age get through such a common experience. What's happened to shape their thinking, so that when the inevitable happens and they are alone, they resolve to get on with it? Like the widow of Russell Hill [who was murdered at his Victorian campsite], *told how she learned to "move on" after the death of her husband and has no hard feelings towards his lover Carol Clay.* How did she learn to *move on* after her husband's unexpected death?[1] Sharing grief can be hard, but what about sharing the practicalities, the realities of living in the time that follows? Brigit and I found quite different paths, but some very similar experiences. Even though it happens every day, it's not in our culture to talk about it and if we do, then somehow it is a reflection that we are not coping with reality. But there's much more than managing the finances, the household and various previously shared tasks. And we need to discuss it.

My friend Lizzie told me about her feelings when she was suddenly alone. She spoke of the loneliness after her long and loving relationship with her partner of 56 years ended, without any warning. They'd had many wonderful adventures over those years; they discussed the practical details of every undertaking, and they enjoyed doing things together. To all their friends, it was clear that they knew each other well. Then, after some years living alone, she moved in with a man she'd known a long time during her marriage. Had she been younger, few would have expected her decision needed an explanation. As an older woman however, many expected her to explain her behaviour – and it wasn't just her family. As a long-term friend, she commented to me: *I liked having a man in my bed. I liked the smell of his body.* Another friend, missing the joy her partner brought to her life, said, rather wistfully: *he made me laugh a lot.* He was a largely self-contained person who encouraged her to continue life with, and through, her close friends. When she was invited to accompany a group of friends who were taking on an adventure style holiday, he knew it wasn't for him but urged her to *go darling, you'll enjoy it.* His instant confirmation of something dear to her told of years of shared pleasure in their lives. And then we were all left on our own.

It was different again for another friend, Cassandra. *My husband died young from an aggressive cancer. We'd been soul mates and loved each other. Life on my own was never what I wanted. Eventually, I met a couple of men who appealed to me, and for a time we enjoyed being together. But I look back and realise I was always comparing the men with my husband. And, in my heart, no one could replace what my husband and I had in common. I do enjoy male company, and I have many women friends.* Like me, she too continued to yearn for something that only another close relationship could satisfy. It was something she too had to keep to herself. Until I asked, that is.

After decades of being on her own, Brigit reflected on her experience following the accidental death of her husband when she was in her forties: *Everybody will have different coping strategies for not being alone… putting the radio on to fill the deafening stillness of an empty house, phoning friends, creating a new routine of life and melding an old one into it. It takes continued effort to take such agency in a time of stunned listlessness, but it's necessary if you don't want to be alone. Others remember you are on your own for a while, but then they expect you to manage your own life again... by yourself.* Who could we tell? It took some years for Brigit to come to terms with this, *being alone and the deep loneliness stemming from the lack of intimacy.* But, she explained, *It takes time to be able to emotionally accept that your former relationship is physically over and can never return. It takes time to not feel guilty about wanting to be held. It takes time to understand that the heart has many rooms, and that your partner will always be in his no matter how many other doors you open.* For others, their response can be dramatic. A few newspaper reports of extreme reactions are not part of this story; they happen, many are true, but they don't shed much light on real life for most women. How does knowledge of only extreme reactions affect the understanding of life for the rest of us, the more widely shared, what can only be described as a typical experience?

From a small sample of women I know, I've learnt that women of all ages have their inner yearnings, and their need for touch and intimacy, and this goes on despite grief. It's unspoken, even with close friends who can recall the feelings of aloneness and isolation Brigit and I experienced. We felt we were expected to deal with our new life, and the less we said about what was missing, the better everyone around us felt. We are praised for stoicism, for coping so well. That is until one of us starts the conversation, and then we learn we are not alone. For most of us, our partners' deaths spelt the death of our social lives even though our inner lives continued. We learned to cope with daily needs, but all our group found ourselves very isolated with our need for intimacy, our need which became a craving for the pleasurable touch of a loving hand.

We'd all lived in the suburbs, the communities where families and couples predominate, and we all know how being alone can mean being isolated inside our houses. And we very quickly learned that women living alone have fewer options for socialising – older women especially. Not just a cup of tea in the afternoon, but the kind of interactions we'd enjoyed as couples, and especially having male company. I will come back to this issue later.

I've learned from friends how the want, the need, and even the craving for an intimate touch, endures. Touch and affection can transform our outlook no matter how limited the intimate moments are. Baring our bodies for a masseur is simply not comparable with the anticipation of the touch of a special other, and an intimate moment. And there's evidence that *social touch is essential to our mental well-being.*[2] But is this confined to those who are in a recognised relationship? Margot, with a few friends, *visited bars and various dating sites…but was disappointed.* There was something missing which she summed up as, *rapport and shared philosophies.* And then she met Malcolm, who had also *given up actively looking for a partner.* Their story has a happy ending, but is it an experience which most, or even many, older women can relate to? They were both single and had a passion in common – their cars - which they could talk about. The passion they excited in each other was less well understood because they were both older people and lived in a centre designed for people at their stage of life. They are both articulate, well-informed people who had separately searched for a partner. But are they typical of how older people fare in their newly single lives? Who would know?

Well-known sex worker and advocate, Julie Bates, told me about a 90-year-old man who lived in aged care and was unsettled and often agitated. So, his family engaged her to visit him. Those were the only intimate details of her encounter that she shared with me, but I was interested in how the unsettled behaviour of an old man living in the isolation of his room in aged care disappeared once his needs for sexual expression were met. As the numbers of older people, women especially, are expected to balloon in coming years, it's a priority for care givers to know what's typical before they can begin to cater to individual needs.

A relationships adviser has posed the danger of isolation and absence of touch and intimacy, leading to anxiety.[3] According to the research done in other countries, the combination of living alone and the absence of the touch of a special other can have deleterious effects. I return to venturing online in the search for a companion in chapter 5. For now, it's looking at how women of all ages, especially older ones, must move beyond trying to socialise face-to-face when opportunities simply disappear. And I include my own experience and those of others in this potentially dangerous new social space, the internet. We all ventured into the unknown, but not for the first time. We're older but being from the change agent generation, we all agree it's a relief to find we are no longer seen as radical; instead, we've become typical. So, what makes us older women tick? I'll work through the answer to this question, next.

Chapter 2

Our secret lives

Ava

I enrolled on a widely advertised and well-known site which was expensive, but I thought it would be safer and have a better chance of success as there is a comprehensive enrolment process. I met 5 or 6 men over a one-year period. They were all lovely men and carefully screened. I felt safe and took no risks. Most of the men were lonely and interested in meeting a woman, but they had very little skill in moving forward. Some suffered guilt as they were widowers; wives mostly had died five or more years previously. Some had created busy lives around giving service to adult families and grandchildren. A couple had created lives around a *good cause*. One man was lovely. We had a very enjoyable afternoon, but we agreed regrettably, there was no chemistry between us.

I met Alex on another well-known site, he replied to my initial entry in minutes. We met, we both had a sense of excitement and chemistry. He was almost too good to be true – therein lies a warning. We quickly moved into a sexual relationship which was wonderful for us both. Four to five months later he had a panic attack and bailed out; he felt *anxiety of commitment*. He said that this was mostly his pattern, unable to commit. We ended the relationship. I was shattered, I went into a classic grief response, which stunned my family, who remained mostly silent and watched me carefully. I think life-long monogamy is not realistic. I would consider a relationship with a married man. I have flirted with two married men but have not taken it any further.

Sophie

I'm a leftover of the 1970s in more ways than one. I met up with women my age, and they seemed to know the main problems for women. And they had good ideas about how to tackle them. That's how I got into community life. And now we look back and are proud of the changes our generation made. I know I am one of the lucky ones, as my husband and I had a good life and relationship. It was so good we even had a daring adventure and came through it in one piece! It was very much part of the era of change. We had a short-term experience with partner exchange. I look back on this now and am amused by how society described it in that era: wife-swapping. And it engages me as, in our case, the *wife-swapping* was driven by the wife of the other couple. I was the last to realise what was happening – she was that kind of self-confident woman. The other man and I were not carried away by it. We enjoyed it at the time.

My husband and I learned later this behaviour was not a novel experience for them. My reaction was mainly about the excitement of doing something like this with my husband's approval. Although I realised that there was a strong sexual attraction between my husband and the woman, even so, perhaps foolishly, I never felt our relationship was under threat. I always felt secure in our relationship, and it never crossed my mind that my husband would leave me. It seems odd now as I look back on this experience.

***

Garcia Marquez[4] made this intriguing observation: *everyone has three lives: a public life, a private life, and a secret life.* I have a public life and a private one. Sharing my secret life with a friend made us think about our other friends, and sure enough, many of them also have a secret life which they were happy to share. Why has it been kept a secret when we all know about it? How have women been persuaded to keep their feelings, their yearnings to themselves as though there is something abnormal about continuing to yearn for the comfort and satisfaction we get from an intimate partner? The Australian Bureau of Statistics (ABS) identifies economic data about older women, the number older than 70, those who own houses etc. But nothing about how we live. So, after 70, it implies that how older women live is of no importance as far as the public, and publicly available information about their lives, is concerned. Then there's the reality that intimacy and desire among grieving people is something we all need to not only know about but to feel comfortable discussing it with others. Being told to get a dog or take up gardening to help cope with mourning the loss of a loved partner is not much help when the profound need is for intimacy and desire. The newly widowed, regardless of age should not need to explain that they had a sex life until not long before the death of their partner. Psychologists confirm that it's *normal for people to miss sex and intimacy with a dying or recently deceased partner* and acknowledge that *friends and therapists may find it uncomfortable to initiate a discussion about sex after widowhood.*[5] And to add to the normality of the need for an intimate other, *scientists have worked out why hugs feel good.*[6] Professional guides for coping with life alone address a number of mental health issues and how to avoid isolation, without a mention of sexual function.[7]

I'm questioning not just whether the secret life of older women relates to our sexuality, but also why it is not widely understood to be part of life as normal for those of us who are ordinary women. Researching information, particularly about older women, helps us understand this about ourselves. It's never been confirmed that women stop needing a special *other* in their lives. But if it's not recognised and not in our conversations, then we're left to feel it is just us. For women like Margot, who've *had a satisfying and enjoyable sex* life, the sudden onset of solo living leaves us isolated and feeling we are alone. I've moved beyond this isolation, and my search includes the internet; it's a familiar part of daily life, we routinely use it for communication, investigation, and socialising. So, what else do we use the internet for? A friend, Ava, had no hesitation in sharing her experience about seeking online for an *other* for intimacy and pleasure. She was surprised to find that some of the men she met *suffered guilt as they were widowers*. Guilt because they were looking to replace the comfort they derived from sharing intimacy with a partner.

In conversation with older women about their need for touch and intimacy I realised I'd touched the surface of a big issue: sexual needs and ageing. It's not the sort of thing that many of us have discussed with others, not even some of our close friends; there's a kind of barrier amongst my contemporaries when it comes to our sexuality. It seems as though we hardly admit it to ourselves. But once I started asking questions, I discovered something else: my contemporaries' sense of being invisible, and this is backed up by scientific study. I acknowledge it's a limited sample of older women but it's the recurring similarities in their responses which intrigued me. With their permission, I wrote down their comments. Many of them, like these from Sophie, were enlightening. *I've had the chance to experience the pleasure of a new relationship again. What really surprised me is that the excitement and sexual arousal are as intense as they were when I was young. So, I thought some things don't change as we get older, despite how most women are seen when they reach their 70s. Added to the excitement is knowing what I am doing. Better late than never!* Another woman, Jane, now in her 80s, added: *So, when the unexpected happened, having a sexual encounter in my 80s, I was very excited. After all, I was getting used to being old, and, like everyone else, I'd accepted that there wasn't much left to find out, especially about myself. There was no one I could talk to now that I was alone after my husband died. I never thought I would write about it. But I can say that my body is very alive to my new partner. We meet infrequently as it's a secret relationship. I do wonder if that also adds to the pleasure.*

In our Australian culture, we learn not to talk about our feelings early in life, especially our sexual ones. Sadly, it is still happening as Katrina Marson describes in her book about the life-long harm done to children, when the sense of shame is associated with sexual expression.[8] When asked to reflect on their personal growth as sexual beings, my sample of women said they had never discussed more than how to respond to menstruation. Few even knew how it was linked to reproduction until they were adolescents. Even then, the available publications were predominantly about sexually transmitted diseases. It's as though sexuality didn't exist. In 2017, Sydney artist Alli Sebastian Wolf devised a scale model of a clitoris to raise awareness of female sexuality, saying *It's really interesting to me just how few people know about how the clitoris works, or what it looks like. I personally didn't know until I was in my mid-20s, which seems like just such a shame.*[9] Dr Wendy Vanselow and others touched on sexuality and older women in a podcast where they discussed a book by Professor Cassandra Szoeke, *Secret of Women's Healthy Ageing: Living Better, Living Longer.*[10] The book is based on a decade-long study of over 400 Australian women in their mid to later years. As late as 2021, on ABC radio this work was described as unique. How the audience responded, well, I don't know. Despite the predominance of older people, especially older women in the ABC radio audience, Professor Szoeke's findings did not become the subject of further conversations. And the work was not of interest to the print media which is the other platform where older women get their information. Renowned chef, Stephanie Alexander, shared some of what she'd learned about life on her own. In a frank and expansive conversation with a journalist, 80-year-old Stephanie said, after 20 years living alone, that *companionship and intimacy are both fantastic things to have, and they seem to be vital to being a happy person.*[11]

As one of a fast-growing number of women who will spend years living alone, I agree. The main reason is longevity. The length of life is one thing, but assumptions about *how* we live during these years – including our sex lives – are quite another. This is particularly relevant to beliefs – and prejudices – about our sexuality.

Many older women – some still in the paid workforce - have no difficulty managing their finances; they are comfortable with computers and using online resources to manage their lives well into old age. To family and friends, it looks impressive; the results can be quantified and observed – diet, exercise, property maintenance, social activities and getting around. But the prevalence of unmet needs for touch and intimacy is unknown. Physical health can be observed, quantified and managed, while mental health of older women remains largely unexplored by researchers.

Some 1,500 participants in a United Kingdom study in 2021, told researchers their stories and experiences demonstrating how deprivation of intimate touch from close family and partners was associated with worse feelings of anxiety and loneliness.[12] A recent US study backs this up by focusing on the power of social touch in reducing stress and pain.[13] Then there's the revelation that having a confidante to share concerns of any kind help shield against dementia.[14] These studies tell us something about how older people live in cultures not unlike Australia. But, there are significant differences between Australia and its northern hemisphere counterparts in how we live, how we express ourselves and how we are governed. All these differences tell us we simply cannot use social research from other countries to know our own community, let alone older women. With my friends, I believe that our society would benefit from more discussion to inform us more broadly. The evidence suggests there are four needs for good overall quality of life. Briefly, it includes:

- Psychological, that is, thinking positive thoughts and having good self-esteem,

- Physical, taking care of the physical body with good sleep hygiene, managing pain, staying mobile, taking prescribed medication, and generally maintaining body weight,

- Environmental, having a safe home, maintaining finances, information, leisure, and,

- Social relationships, keeping old friendships and maintaining intimate relationships, including sex, plus social support from the wider community.[15]

In recent times, there's been an avalanche of comments and opinions in the daily media about some or all these points. So, some 60-plus years ago, when I was growing up, I looked back at what was in the public domain that helped shape my generation's self-awareness and knowledge about how our bodies functioned? How we came to know what was expected of us as young women. It wasn't hard to identify what boy's roles were in our society, but what about young women? What did we know and where did we learn it? Was there a single source of information beyond our family group? I'll explain.

Chapter 3

What did we expect of life?

Motherhood is the only option.

A country girl's experience

Margot

Then I met Malcolm. He'd been married happily for over 45 years. He'd tried internet dating after his wife died. He also read books about sex and internet dating. He was enjoying cycling and had given up actively looking for a partner. Malcolm is 80 and has health problems endemic to men of his age. When we first met, he had to go into hospital for erectile dysfunction (ED) and his urologist prescribed an injection. It helps him to get an erection but it's difficult to maintain – he didn't find *Viagra* useful.

Together we visited the local sex shop – it's part of a chain that is owned by a woman and run by women who all know the products and what they can do. We purchased a cock ring and that, combined with the injection, enables him to have a good erection that lasts for probably 20-30 minutes. I was happy to find that Malcolm is one of those rare men who can give me an orgasm (without intercourse). He knows about a woman's clitoris, where it is and what to do with it. He explained that he'd read about it. At the beginning of our relationship, my dormant sexuality suddenly went ballistic and my whole body was in a constant state of sexual excitement for a few months which was amazing. I hadn't had so many orgasms since I was first married. Thank goodness it has settled down a lot after 12 months of us sleeping together. At our age, we've learnt that sex is very different from when we were younger. Although Malcolm has been able to have and maintain an erection with the aid of the injection and cock ring, he has not had an orgasm since we met. This has worried me a bit because it seems that I am getting all the pleasure. He seems sanguine about it because of what he has read about the problems of sex for older men, but he does still enjoy the feeling of intercourse with me. He says he also gets great pleasure from my orgasms and the intimacy of lying naked together and feeling my breasts on his chest.

***

Before I get back to the sexuality of older women and how it has evolved to where it is today, I'll explain that I began my life in regional New South Wales; I was an adult when I moved to live in Sydney. It does seem that some metropolitan populations may have provided a larger world view for young women's lives, but the evidence is hard to find beyond a few individual experiences. In smaller regional populations, social mores are much easier to identify, and the role of print media, especially the Australian Women's Weekly [AWW],[16] in preserving these influences. Before the 1970s my life typifies the social isolation of most women and men at that time. For pre-internet youth, there was no identifiable time of *adolescence* – that came in the 1970s when young people got jobs and were targets for advertising. By 1970 I was ripe for city life and had the chance to be involved in the epoch-making change in women's lives, something not possible in the regions back then. In the city, teaming up with other change agents, my enjoyment of the anonymity of Sydney life, and the opportunities which came with tertiary education, are my story. And my story parallels the epoch-making changes the Women's Movement introduced.

In the rules-dominated era of the 1960s in country NSW, I worked in a bank when a bank job was considered a more respectable workplace for young women than say, work in retail. Young women working in a factory was never discussed. In banks back then, only tellers handled money, and only men became tellers. Women of all ages had to content themselves with administration and secretarial roles. When one of my colleagues said to me, *I've got a new job,* I could hardly take it in, even though it was in the same town. The pay was so much better; it entailed shorter hours because it was at the local factory. She had the courage to take the job. I say courage because it did not have instant social prestige and, therefore, social acceptance that the bank job carried. Same tasks, fewer hours – banks still opened on Saturday mornings whereas factories did not - and the pay and conditions were better. It took social control to keep divisions like this in place.

My bank job came to an end when I married. In my friendship circles, it was the general expectation that I would leave the paid workforce once I became a wife. It took coming to the city for me to discard convention and seek paid employment after a decade at home with our three children. Why? Because in country towns, women from the professions – medicine, law, accountancy, teaching etc – could continue in their paid employment without it reflecting adversely on their husband's ability to support their families. Not so for other areas such as retail and secretarial - the main opportunities for women who did not have tertiary education. I was one of them, and I was not alone. Even now, the smaller the population, the more challenging it is to modernise social rules, especially when they are unspoken. And, it almost goes without saying, especially when the rules relate to women's behaviour.

My good life started in the tumultuous 1970s. I go into this in the next chapter. For now, some four decades later, I return to the day I realised I was seen as old, and I was alone. My partner of 60 years had died. It wasn't age that shocked me, but living without a companion, without touch, without intimacy. That's when it dawned on me that how women feel living without the touch of an *other* is a secret. It is not something older women feel comfortable talking about. That is, until someone bravely broaches the subject, like journalist Benjamin Law did with Stephanie Alexander. She offered insights she'd gained, including during her time in Paris, and its enjoyment of all things sensual: *I go along with the notion of food as being intrinsically sexy...[it] can certainly work up an atmosphere. In fact, one of the special occasions I do remember – linked with romance for me, in Paris – was having an assignation, which was improper...it was pretty wicked. He was somebody else's husband.*

In this instance, I'm curious to know why the flouting of convention is more shocking, and headline grabbing, than knowing there is an enduring need for intimacy? The latter was not picked up by anyone. Why, I ask, is a mutually satisfying, not uncommon experience regarded as improper at best, and wicked at worst? It's not just how our media operates, it's also how older women behave, how they are persuaded to keep their innermost needs and desires to themselves. It's a feature of our culture, and it's not new; it's simply not recognised. Just how did our society come to understand that there is a cut-off date for these feelings? How did we persuade older women to go along with this? It turns out it's a gradual process beginning with not talking about it, right through to references to *older* - meaning women in their seventies and onwards - and fostering only negative images of what it is to be old. How did we come to believe that ageing meant loss of the ability to experience sensual pleasure. Why do we expect that the death of a partner is accompanied by the death of the need for a partner? Cartoonists have routinely depicted older women as dehydrated, often toothless hags, symbols which entertain younger people while reinforcing something that is simply not true, that being an older woman means living in a body which lacks vigour, joy and meaning. It's just not true but then how would anyone other than individual older women, know anything different?

So, back to the 1970s, what changed our relationships forever? I'm one of the lucky ones who benefited from the reliability of the contraceptive pill, and the revolution it helped bring about. Social researchers like Hugh Mackay thought it underpinned the two aspects of the most significant social revolution of the 1970s – namely the pill and the women's movement.[17] As leading feminist, Anne Summers, explained how it was for a young single woman with an unplanned pregnancy. *The shame was scarifying, and it too often meant that life's options quickly closed. University plans had to be shelved; other dreams abandoned. There were three choices: a shotgun marriage to the boy, who might be someone you scarcely knew and did not even like; having it which meant being bundled off to a home for unmarried mothers and usually being forced to give up the baby for adoption. There was no supporting mothers' benefit then, no way to raise a child without family support. And, unlike today, few families welcomed their unwed daughter's pregnancy.*[18] A big positive for women like me, we knew we could get paid work, and with higher education, be confident we could commit to the timetables needed. It's hard to imagine the era before safe, reliable, accessible contraception was widely available to women. Its effect was personal; it was political, and it made good economic sense. The way it profoundly affected women's confidence was remarkable; importantly, it ensured a woman's income could be relied on to pay the mortgage. Not that this was formally recognised, because women like me were told directly that our *earnings could not be considered, because we might get pregnant.* An old trope which banks hung onto but it would not exclude us from the paid workforce. The contraceptive pill was not only a revolution in women's lifetimes. It changed the world.

The absence of reliable birth control was one thing restricting women's choices. The other is the role of religious organisations. It's hard to imagine how restrictive some forms of religion were, especially on women's decision-making. And that was before waves of migration from non-Judeo-Christian ethnicities[19] brought different belief systems to Australia. Belief systems which deter women from using birth control are hard to counter and continue to determine so much about women's lives. The widespread support for changes introduced in the 1970s has waxed and waned over the years. When our daughters completed their education, the jobs they wanted were open to them, so they saw no reason to campaign as their mothers had. Even today, young women are ill prepared for the orchestrated, intrusive political campaigns which aim to limit women's autonomy over their bodies. When women's roles and their potential professional development is constrained, women are denied the opportunity to be full members of society. But not everyone was convinced, like the doctor writing in 1982 who blamed it for *an increase in permissiveness.*[20]

This did not apply to Margot and her experiences symbolises the major social changes ushered into Australian society by the contraceptive pill and the women's movement. After...*a satisfying and enjoyable sex life in marriage,* she did not enjoy life without it after her husband left. She had no idea where to look for a partner, so she joined some friends and *visited bars and various dating sites...but was disappointed.* She could not have done that easily before the birth control pill became available to women. Very few of her married friends included her in their social gatherings. But when her husband decided to end the marriage, he left and immediately *moved in with a woman with whom he was working.* Margot, freed from the tyranny of unwanted pregnancy, found there was time and energy to start looking and questioning our generation's attitudes and actions. Margot was one of many who recognised the need for change in women's lives to reflect our changing times.

In all eras, social mores are succinctly reflected in the lyrics of popular music. A song, launched in 1970 and popular for the following decade, titled, *In the Summertime,* spoke for the times: *If her daddy's rich take her out for a meal / If her daddy's poor just do what you feel.* In the internet age and its widely used social media platforms, it's hard for current generations to believe how much has changed about most aspects of life for women. It may come as a shock for young women contemplating marriage today to know that it was commonplace till mid last century for women to promise to *obey* their partner. In the 1960s, a married woman could not seek tubal ligation without her husband's written permission. It is particularly interesting to remember that at that time, it was not routinely acceptable for young people to live together before marriage. But the high rate of pregnancy amongst women at the time of their marriage in the pre-1970s era, helps us understand the impact of safe, reliable birth control, available to women.

Assumptions about the lives of older women today are one thing, but evidence, the lived experience, is better. It may shock some to learn that women's need for choice about their social life, their preferences and sense of themselves, does not diminish with age. That's why I'm raising the subject of sexuality - intimacy and touch - so that other women can begin a discussion, hopefully one which will stimulate researchers to gather up-to-date evidence of their lived experiences. Research samples need to be large to demonstrate and accommodate the breadth of how older women express their wants and needs for intimacy. And this will go some way to replace current assumptions which are regularly based on attitudes and norms from bygone eras.

Back before the internet was invented, when I was growing up, the term *proper behaviour* was in vogue. So, long before the internet and a raft of influencers came along, conventional norms – many unchanged from my parents' era – dictated how girls and women were expected to behave. And there was no more widely shared platform for guidance than the Australian Women's Weekly (AWW); it was the standard bearer for advice and benchmarks to all women regardless of their differing circumstances. There were no exceptions, no grey areas. A brief digression to mention the work of Norman Haire, who was a sexologist writing for women in the 1940s and challenging many attitudes and beliefs about sexuality generally, and in particular women's health.[21] It appears that post-war, the priority to increase the population took precedence over women's sexuality as a topic popular in mainstream media. Norman Haire's findings were virtually unknown for several decades after he published his ground-breaking research.

Back to the AWW and the tenor of its advice. Iron-clad certainty makes for easy reading, unlike its effect and the burden being placed on women who were compelled to live by the rules it dictated. A glance through some of the letters from the 1930s to the 1960s demonstrates the style championed by the AWW. The print media era when the views of a very few were broadcast and simultaneously received by the many, plus the power of certainty which characterises the AWW, is enjoyed only by fringe groups in the internet age. The best letters were paid for. Back in 1938, one headed *Bachelor Girls* was about women in their twenties working in offices, trying to tell themselves *that they have not reached the time for marriage.* It then reminded readers that *the wives and mothers of this generation, as of every other, are, for the most part, the ones who marry early.* It was a reminder that women could suffer the worst fate for a woman, that of missing out on marriage and motherhood. At this time, the Australian population was just under seven million having grown by less than a million in a decade after WWI, evidence of the combined impacts of world war and economic depression.

The tendency to prolong youth among women featured in another letter on the same page in the AWW. It was headed *Unnatural* and explained that women could use this to *shirk the responsibility which is theirs to build a home…as soon as they reached womanhood…*because the *prolongation of youth brings no real happiness, and women who try to indulge in it miss the joy that comes to a youthful wife and mother.*[22] It could hardly be clearer to women that they had a primary role no matter what else may interest them. Then, twenty years later in 1958, a woman regretted a faux pas about thinking a child's lovely clothes and curly hair signified it was a girl - the indignant mother quickly put the record straight, and said the child was a boy. It was a mistake so distressing that the poor misunderstood admirer, *wished the earth had swallowed me and that all mothers would cut their sons' hair and make them masculine.*[23] Regimenting women's behaviour and appearance was quite possibly a hangover from the war years. Men went along with it with haircuts known as *short back and sides,* and mothers were keen to show their son's aspiration to become a man. The haircut was step one. Almost without comment, as war drained the available male workforce, women responded to the call to take on work previously the preserve of men, such as in factories and manufacturing, and farm hands doing agricultural and domestic work. Individually and collectively, it seems everyone knew women could do unpaid work at home and paid work outside the home, at the same time.

The socially defining role of the AWW reached all ages. Teenagers sought guidance for approved behaviour, like the

15-year-old wanting to know about being, …*old enough to wear make-up, earrings, and high-heeled shoes* and being *old enough to go to balls.* The advice was crisp and clear: *You are old enough to wear a little pink lipstick when you go out, but not old enough for earrings or high-heeled shoes or to go to balls.*[24] In the same 1958 edition, the editor was deluged with replies from women about *what attracted the opposite sex.* And, while some men - how many is not known – wrote to the women's publication, they used only a few words. The editor concluded that *nearly all women believed it was important to boost a man's ego;* but *few men agreed – or were willing to say so.*[25] The AWW was not strong on balancing a range of viewpoints. In that era, evidence of the lived experience of women of any age is very hard to find. Family histories detail how women were occupied but few reveal very much how women felt about their lives.

Then two things happened which changed the nation and the course of life for the majority of women. I have already dealt with one: accessible, affordable and safe contraception. The other was yet to come.

Chapter 4

WEL and activism

Everything in the world is about sex except sex. Sex is about power.

Oscar Wilde

WEL

A small but eager group of volunteers gathered in the Grosvenor Street WEL office in the early 1980s; most of us yet to take our place in the paid workforce. At the height of our activism, we were all busy caring for our families, and some were continuing with study programs. The office was made available to us by a generous benefactor, Stella Cornelius, a noted businesswoman at the time. We all worked as many hours as we could manage on two to three days a week. Pam Simons worked all the time, at home, on holidays, when she woke in the evenings. She was a mainstay. We gathered stories from individuals to build case studies and, with a bit of help, wrote legislation to put our case to government as we appealed for support.

The era of dramatic changes, brought about by the social upheaval of the 1970s in NSW, is part of the story of The Women's Electoral Lobby [WEL]. Its proponents, its defenders, and, ultimately, the community of women which developed in relatively few years, were at the heart of many changes; and, in some significant areas, WEL was a leader of the change. Thanks to the epoch-making reforms of the Whitlam government, many of us were mature age students in higher education through 1970s and 80s. We gained skills and formed many new friendships which continued for the remainder of our lives.

***

The story of empowerment and women's sexuality are closely linked in the public sphere. We know very little about how it was experienced in women's private lives; and, beyond their fertile years there is practically nothing on record. No surprise that society, culture, legislation, medicine and religion have concurred to present individual needs according to convention, control and values. Women like me know we need intimacy, but seldom control the how, where and when it can be satisfied. We know that, in the main, women live longer than men. Soon there will be more older people than young, and they will mostly be women. So why do we older women have to grapple with sexist and ageist stereotypes based on little more than myths and legends? There's more: after menopause, not only do we older women experience a sense of being absent from the public eye, but, if we are mentioned, it is frequently in a negative way - asexual and lacking hormonal activity. These descriptions influence how society views and obstructs, and even damages women's emotional, physical and sexual health.

It goes back to what we heard about when we were no longer children, but not yet qualified to be adults. Eligibility to vote, getting a driver's licence came with reaching the age of 21. When we were adolescents – for the generations who are in their 70s and older, transition to adulthood pre-dated the very word adolescent – the word was not part of our everyday language. As the 1970s, post school/young adult generation began earning, and were free to spend their earnings as they wished, the advertising industry was quick to offer them things they could buy. And the term *adolescent* quickly came to refer to this age group. But I hasten to add, getting on with life in our older years in today's world, is not comparable with our experience of transitioning from teenage to young adult. Back then, we just got on with it, we didn't talk about it. Come to think of it, we didn't talk about much else that was happening in our lives, at a time when our sexuality was as present in our minds as it is for today's adolescents.

So, what changed? It was the 1970s - the pivotal time of change in Australia – when women of all ages seized the chance to demand recognition of them as people, their place in society and eventually, their individuality.[26] Aah, the 70s and social ferment. No wonder older Australian women often just sigh and cast their minds back to a time when social change was the order of the day. It was happening on many fronts but the one which concerns us now, was the engine room of change, in Sydney: The Women's Electoral Lobby.[27] It began in a relatively small way, without funds, but with energetic and enthusiastic women who were unsure of their capacity to affect change, all bursting with ideas for a better way forward. It was when women in WEL catalogued the systematic discrimination in how people related to each other as well as to employers, and to government. As we focused on the need for systematic change in services dedicated to women, WEL was joined by other women's groups including Women's Liberation Movement, female run health centres, rape crisis centres, the women's refuge movement, and women behind bars.

There's more detail about the WEL I joined, and some of my experiences in the WEL office, in Appendix 2. Research evidence plus the experiences of people who wrote to us and some, who came into the WEL office to tell us, made it possible to identify what was systematic misuse of female participation in the paid workforce. The phrase is a mouthful, but it is important to distinguish between paid and unpaid work which women performed. It was not easy to ignore the push-back we got from men and women, in our immediate, as well as wider, communities. Not everyone could find a light-hearted way to bring the matter to everyday conversation the way a friend's husband did. A fellow office worker proudly stated that his wife didn't work, to which her husband replied: *you'd better get her fixed.*[28] Some men as well as women, began to look closely at the language in use and the meaning it was intended to convey. We had to argue that the word *man* was not used to convey a sense of inclusiveness, it did not automatically convey to women that they were included along with men, in either conversation or legislation. It took persistence in the face of men calling for us to *lighten up*. Anti-female humour was equally as difficult to ignore or discuss. And the word *feminist* was seldom used alone; most preferring to qualify it with *radical* to add emphasis or show disapproval. That is how many of us experienced our new category.

After I graduated, I continued as a part time worker in the WEL office for a time. WEL activists were moving on to become trailblazers in the toughest area of all to make change, the public sector. The community got used to the image of men in management and leadership roles. Women, before they could take on these roles, had to convince government and the community that they could do the job. But, to their credit, women like Helen L'Orange, Alison Ziller and Jozefa Sobski, stepped into leadership roles in small units within existing public service structures,[29] and quickly made them not only effective, but also acceptable platforms for introducing policy changes. In these roles, they had to be resolute and fearless in the face of often well-crafted obstacles, to any change. Looking back, it seems obvious that opposition would come from within a system that had been dominated, almost exclusively, by men. The natural justice of the issues women argued, was entrenched belief in what had always been normal, that men lead. The different perspectives women could bring to public life is a concept which has been slow to entrench in people's minds and in public discussion. We always acknowledged the immense debt women owed to the enlightened leadership of Premier Neville Wran who built around him a cabinet of Ministers who agreed with his priorities. Men like Peter Anderson, Minister for Health, and Rodney Cavalier, Minister for Education.

I'd never been to a public demonstration of group solidarity until the International Women's Day marches became a regular fixture in our calendar. Marching in the streets! It was an all new experience for most of us, and in no small part, made possible because of the anonymity of city life. And it was for a cause which bound us together in our new-found awareness of the systematic nature of cultural attitudes and practices which had a detrimental effect on everyone's lives whether they recognised it or not. It was sexism. We needed to push back. And we continue to need to push back as we discover how discriminatory attitudes and behaviour persist in our culture. Outbreaks of right-wing political movements – on full display in the USA in the lead up to the 2024 presidential election - continue to include a goal of returning women to a culture which defines them by their biological capabilities, not the goals and ambitions of autonomous beings.

Discrimination and the consequent negative attitudes towards women continue to permeate society in Australia today. For instance, older women and men alike, experience a sense of being *invisible,* of feeling alone in multi-generational gatherings for instance. It's something that links us to younger women also, some in their forties, who believe it happens to them. It's a form of discrimination which binds generations of women just like the gender pay gap does. I'm putting the focus on how history, sex education generally, and society have influenced women to accept the reality of what continues as a sort of secret life – our ongoing need for an *other.* I am a fifth-generation Australian, raised in regional Australia and I came to Sydney in 1970. My own actions and those of my friends represent real life, then and now. And we are not keeping it to ourselves although few older women get the chance a couple of high-profile men, who are approaching retirement age, did with half a page in a newspaper to express their exasperation.[30]

It's not true that in previous decades, all women subscribed to the belief that women's destiny is motherhood. For instance, the daughters who grew up with mothers who were professional women – in the law, medical and business – knew there were other ways to use their lives. But, as revealed in the pages of the Australian Women's Weekly [AWW] in the following chapter, even they were made to feel that motherhood was normal for them before any other lifestyle.[31] There's always been whole groups, including many lesbians, who have not felt compelled to believe reproducing the species was, or is, their primary purpose in life. This story is about what was, and continues to be, typical for women.

What came under question had previously not been discussed by women, was and is about their lived experience. The Women's Movement comprised white, mainly middle-class women and did not involve Indigenous women - it was not a deliberate decision – nor was there an intention to exclude others such as migrant women, women who worked in factories, or those on production lines. It took an over-arching movement to establish what was common to the lives of women regardless of social, educational and economic circumstances. It was not common amongst women, regardless of background, to talk about wanting an identity which was separate from that of family life; while talk about their vaginas would have been next to shocking. The more daring sat around with mirrors examining that part of their bodies. They knew about their pubic area, but most had simply never seen it. Then, with mirror in hand plus a few friends, they explored their labia; some had discovered their pubic nerve though they'd not talked about it. A BBC documentary confirmed this to be a common practice even today.[32] As previously mentioned, in 2017 the launch of a huge gold-plated clitoris by a Sydney artist made news in the UK but not in Australia. When the artwork was launched in 2017 at the Sydney Opera House, it was described as *a giant, sparkling clitoris, a 100:1 scale model of the real thing, covered in intricate, sequinned 'nerves' so that it lights up the room 'like a divine disco ball'.* [33] Significantly, with the advent of the pill, sex and sexuality were no longer automatically linked to pregnancy, and I come back to this in more detail in chapter five. This was not a development that was executed clinically, but it did break down barriers to what we knew even if we had not discussed it with other women; and, how we began to understand our bodies, ourselves [there's a book title in that], in greater depth. It's widely recognised that once people experience activism, in all its forms, they seldom relinquish the knowledge of how it works. For a few more decades, most women felt constrained by society to see themselves principally as a mother. The daughters who grew up with mothers who were professional women also knew there were other ways to use their lives. But even they understood that motherhood was considered normal for them before any other lifestyle, as previously discussed. It took the activism of the 1970s to put this widely held notion under the microscope.

We understand the *why* part of the influences which ensured people were aware of their responsibility to society. What is not widely known is the *how* people come to reflect on long held beliefs about women's lives. At the time, influences came from the economy, from government, and, very infrequently, from community groups – groups like WEL. Today, we may wonder why it was an uphill battle for WEL women to get their message out into the public arena; but it's no surprise when we reflect on how they were socialised. And its today's older women – the cohort who were change agents in earlier decades – who are resisting the pressures to quietly fade out of view. WEL would not have been the effective change agent it was had it not been for the widespread support it garnered from women by focusing on the way their lives were impacted by entrenched beliefs, habits and attitudes. WEL appealed to women, in roles and occupations, leading lives that were typical at the time. The information WEL gathered, the questions they asked about women's views and reactions to issues like childcare, health services, employment and the enduring one, the right to choice on pregnancy. The decision makers were not reflecting the lived experiences of women as there were few options for two-way communication in the pre-digital world. Largely, women believed they were alone with their views and insights. That's what WEL found out when women were asked for feedback; women who'd distinguished themselves at the community level; a few high-profile individuals like Elizabeth Reid,[34] through word of mouth, local groups, and, surveys. The WEL survey results, produced using a scorecard, continues to be an effective data gathering device. Today, it's the typical older woman whose experiences and opinions are rarely known. The Older Women's Network has an impressive record in representing the issues affecting older women in NSW.[35] When someone asks.

WEL continues to advocate to government, business, political parties etc for a society that includes equality of opportunity for all. The WEL scorecard, a set of questions put to would be politicians in the lead up to an election, continues to be an effective tool for demonstrating a candidate's understanding and approach to inequality and injustice, as it was decades ago. Individual women in WEL began as typical members of their communities, before their advocacy for change made them stand out from the crowd. Women like former CEO, Family Planning NSW, Margaret McDonald; social scientist, Eva Cox, writer, former academic Juliet Richters; and leading public servants, Anne Summers and Helen L'Orange, are amongst many who have acquired widely known public profiles.[36] To their credit, although they are no longer typical of how women live in society, they haven't given up on the needs of women who have lives which are more typical of older women today.

Despite the admirable efforts of some high-profile women, reaction seems to be only parked and ready to be reactivated. A journalist writing in the Australian media argues that the so-called public debate about the capability of the woman candidate in the US Presidential election has reached an extreme not previously experienced. Also, participation by women in public life now carries a warning about the danger.[37] Reading this sobering assessment, I ask how the social changes to the status of women begun in the 1970s have not translated into permanent change. Why are older women either missing from the media or, if they are featured it's not for what they bring to society. Today's older women emerged in public life during the Women's Movement years. Their lived experience is assumed and is largely devoid of understanding or even respect. How did the heroic achievements of the 1970s and beyond allow ordinary women to go missing to this degree?

Chapter 5

Older women go missing

Language not only communicates emotion but also shapes it[38]

Marion

I am very interested in how other women my age – I'm in my early 80s – continue to want the pleasure I've always had with sex. I have my share of health problems. And I'm keen to follow the rules for getting the most out of life – exercising, eating good food and having an interest that keeps my brain ticking over. It's hard to pick up a newspaper without finding an article that goes over this advice to older people. But I've noticed there is never much talk about our sex lives – none really. So, when the very unexpected happened, having a sexual encounter in my 80s, I was very excited. After all, I was getting used to being *old*, and, like everyone else, I'd accepted that there wasn't much left to find out, especially about myself. There was no one I could talk to now that I'm alone. I never thought I would write about it. But I can say that my body is very alive to my new partner. We meet infrequently as it's what we call an *illicit* relationship – I think that adds to the pleasure.

I'm still getting used to living on my own and find it hard to get back to sleep when I wake in the night. I start going over a few things if I've had a busy day. I don't know where I read it, but someone wrote about using a vibrator – clitoral stimulation is a good distraction! I've only tried it a couple of times, but it does help me relax and get back to sleep. I'm grateful to you for talking about something which matters a lot to me. I also wonder if my experience is not so rare as there aren't many possible partners for women my age.

***

The words we use in public discourse have always mattered. I don't expect an argument about that, but before I focus on the style and precision of wording in the national mouthpiece for Australian women pre-1970s, the Australian Women's Weekly, it is useful to note the continued power of words about the lives of women in the 21st century. Even now, our society has maintained a media image of women and the problems we confront as separate and distinct from the society in which we live. This biased and prejudicial stance is not confined to Australia. It follows that whatever the problem women encounter it's something they have somehow contributed to or caused. For instance, targets to ensure equal representation of women and men in leadership roles – especially in political parties – are being ignored or countered with tired old arguments implying women are the problem or are incapable of cool-headed decision-making. An Australian political party, heavy with male leadership, is often described as having a *woman problem*.[39] Male decision-makers have the power to change the under-representation of women in their organisation, but the language used to describe the situation infers that the problem belongs to women. The problem is seen to be with women, not the society we live in. That won't surprise many people who want domestic violence statistics to be identified as behaviour of perpetrators, and not simply the number of female victims. This reflects a long-held habit of identifying injustice and inequality for women as a woman's problem.[40]

The better results for corporate boards headed or dominated by women during the GFC [global financial crisis] have received very little attention.[41] In some quarters, merit-based female leadership threatens men's sense of what it is to be male. How else to explain the audible groans of male MPs when a female member rose to ask questions about a woman who had suffered a horrific sexual attack? The moans and groans implied the issues had been raised, so now let's move on to more critical governance issues.

Back when the AWW spoke for all women, all women had their place and shared a universal aspiration - marriage and motherhood. Sounds outrageous? For this discussion starter, taking a look at Australian society before our over 70-year-olds were even middle-aged, is useful. We need to consider this notion of universality to understand the significance of social changes in the 1970s. And it helps us understand why older women are largely missing in our media, on screens or in print. Ita Buttrose, recently retired Chair of the Australian Broadcasting Commission [ABC][42] being a notable exception. But it's true, that even though profiles of a few outstanding individuals appear in print media,[43] while others have a special section for those who have undergone obvious plastic surgery to hide the signs of ageing, none of these women could be described as ordinary people or typical of older women in Australia today. The title of a recently published attempt to address the situation, *Cougars Grannies & Old Bags*, supports this conclusion.[44]

Where are the older female program presenters on Australian television? Or, for that matter, presenting radio programs? These are valid questions when we know that older people, predominantly older women, are the main consumers of both print and electronic media in Australia. But our capitalist economy quickly comes to a crucial question: where's the money in older women? Many older people, particularly women, still prefer to listen to the radio. Whether it's magazines or popular television programs it doesn't take long to notice there is very little about the lived experience of older people and particularly, older women. Older women rarely feature in erotic novels or pornography, soft or hardcore. Until now, that is, but the exceptions are few. It takes persistence to go beyond free-to-air television to find films where older women have a younger partner in any endeavour. The 1971 film, Harold and Maude, about a young, rich, and obsessed with death, Harold, finds himself changed forever when he meets lively septuagenarian Maude at a funeral.[45] An older woman and a younger man are still newsworthy for the ages of the parties with little or no reflection on the substance of their relationship. A contemporary of mine, who spent her youth in Europe, made this observation: *I do think we live in a very ageist society where people over sixty are labelled as 'elderly', and therefore not part of mainstream society. European countries on the other hand, have a different approach to their older citizens. They are respected and cherished.*

During my early years it was usual to focus on our appearance and seldom, if ever, on our performance. The effects of this on today's older women is well demonstrated by Emma Thompson in *Good Luck to you, Leo Grande*. She was 62 at the time, and her focus on her body image reflects a reality many older women would relate to. It would take many words for a younger person to attempt to convey the anxiety and uncertainty which Thompson exhibited in her behaviour, but she didn't need words to convey such strong feelings. Older women would instantly share her experience. And pause for a moment to reflect on two more recent articles about women in the media in the US and in Australia and note that words matter. First, Australia and the attention-grabbing headline, *Boobs too big!* Then the article continued: *No wonder women don't go on TV…vile, sexist vitriol…that women with a profile, especially in media or politics, are considered completely fair game for vicious, sexualised or sexually violent personal abuse,*[46] for doing their job. The focus on appearance not performance of women from all backgrounds, applies to women who are in senior and leadership roles, including the Australian Government *e*Safety Commissioner, MPs and journalists. It leads to the observation that according to Curtin/ANU research, this abuse has a *silencing, trickle-down effect.* Women from all public roles hesitate to appear in the media.

Roles for women, in radio or television programs are few, and for older women they are fewer still. Caroline Jones continued her outstanding career well into her older years on ABC platforms,[47] but she is a notable exception. This is a significant difference between Australia and the US. In the latter, many esteemed older journalists, men and women, continue in their profession as public broadcasters. In Australia, a program, formerly on the public broadcaster *SBS*, had a high following among daytime viewers in Australia. It was a US-focused news program, and, at the time, was anchored by 75-year-old Judy Woodruff.[48] In the US today, it is argued that the *pressure to look hot is taking the joy out of getting older*. And it affects men and women.[49] The list of surgical and chemical interventions as well as the fake hair and expensive underwear to achieve the required shape, are all necessary to alter the natural features of both Martha Stewart, 81 and Jane Fonda, 85 for their pin-up appearances. Vast expense and discomfort are necessary to deny and disguise any semblance of ageing naturally. Unfortunately, agencies like the Older Women's Network, while it represents older women in Australian society, does not have the resources to push back against the general Americanisation of Australian culture[50] with its heavy marketing of role models like these women, and the negative image of ageing they perpetuate.

When today's over 70s women in Australia were young and impressionable, attitudes and expectations for their lives, would be barely recognisable today. Which leads me to ask how did we get here? What did we know about how our bodies worked? What were the social forces that made us this way.

Feminism hit the ground running in Sydney and Melbourne, markedly in the 1970s and 80s. The era now recognised as the second Women's Movement, seemed to come from nowhere. Before that, the rules for proper behaviour, spelt out clearly in the *AWW*, went unchallenged. *I think we should go to this meeting,* my friend Ellie said to me in the early 1970s. She was talking about a *WEL* meeting. She'd recently returned from London and witnessed the swing of the 1960s sweep through society there. In contrast, I knew only country life in Australia, where marriage and motherhood were the norm and the expectation. It's hard to go past the role of WEL as a significant catalyst for a major change in how women lived. A few other women's organisations, such as *Women's Liberation*, emerged at this time, and they all agreed on the need for change. I was not alone coming under scrutiny when I opened my own business. It was a busy time, as I was also a part-time university student. Statements like this arose: *I don't know why you bothered to have children; you don't have time for them.* These words from the wife of a guest leaving after a dinner party at my place took me by surprise. It was the late 1970s, and my children were in secondary school – two in the final two years. It was one of many similar rebukes from women and men. Some were simply curious, while others were curious about why I wasn't satisfied with all I had, a husband, children, a house and garden etc. Over dinner one evening, a high-profile neighbour peppered me with questions such as, *why are you angry? why don't you like men? what is wrong with you?* And this was all because of my known involvement in WEL, which had not come up earlier in our conversation that evening.

The 1970s Women's Movement helped change how women live, work and are seen in public life. It was change that was hard won for the majority who pioneered the change – most of us in WEL at the time had established families. Behind the common reaction, was questioning what was wrong with us for wanting more out of life than caring for our family. I note that big changes for lesbian women came a bit later. So how did women's sexuality fit into what became known as the *second wave Women's Movement?* The 1970s Women's Movement also dared focus on the almost unspoken topic, women's sexuality. Back then, women needed to develop language for talking about it, when and how it could be discussed, and at what age. Even now, there is confusion about the difference between *feminine* and *female* as a notice in the women's toilet in a major Sydney hospital demonstrates. The instruction is about where to deposit menstrual products, but the notice describes *feminine hygiene products*. Little wonder we had difficulty introducing language describing behaviour.

Decades ago, the prevailing view was that learning about our bodily and emotional functions would naturally lead to bad behaviour. A now former Member of the NSW Legislative Council,[51] had relied on such fixed attitudes to continue his role in public life for over four decades. He is not alone with repeated attempts to promote notions about relationships and sexual behaviour, that *ignorance is bliss*. The marriage breakdown rate contradicts this notion, and so does other evidence, such as domestic violence. Ignorance was not universally bliss. Significantly, it was almost impossible for women to initiate divorce before the 1975 Family Law Act was enacted. WEL was a driving force in securing this legislation and those of us who were in the WEL office heard some tragic stories of how women who had lived with wealth and privilege, and its accompanying social prestige, were robbed of these advantages once they were divorced. One in particular stands out; her only way of supporting herself was doing housework in a mansion where she had formerly been a guest.

Admittedly, I am drawing on a small sample to question whether we older women continue to think of ourselves as sexual beings. Social policy researcher, Hugh Mackay claimed that, the oral contraceptive pill changed women's lives forever and his conclusions are backed up elsewhere.[52] Women could focus on sex for enjoyment once they were free of the fear of pregnancy. Using the right words has always mattered. So, the question arises, what language – spoken or written – can older women in Australia use for their personal lives as they age? And when do older women begin to think about their individual yearnings, both sexual and a desire for intimacy and touch? Is there an age when women stop wanting this pleasure. I didn't have to be hyper-sensitive about the image of older women in the publications I looked at – especially the daily print media – to note that just about all references to women and ageing have given it a negative image, including denying natural physical change, especially about appearance. Few publications even mentioned older women and those that did, they had only negative images of older women's sexuality. It's a reasonable conclusion that, if it's not in our language, it's not shared. Certainly not outside most people's small personal networks. Younger people cannot accurately represent the inner feelings, wants and desires of older people. They may read statistical data, but it is not the same as heeding an older woman speaking about the needs of older women. And when we ask older women about their lived experiences, as I have done, then we are likely to get new, up to date information which has not previously been identified. Nowhere is this more relevant than attitudes towards sex. And it's even more relevant when the conversation is about women in their seventies and eighties.

It's time to ask where we are up to now? Women like Ronni Kahn, AO, CEO of the food rescue charity Oz Harvest, is an outstanding woman, is a trail-blazing philanthropist and deserves all the publicity she gets. But she is not representative of women over 60, and how they live, work and present themselves in society. An example of one does not disprove a rule which applies to women generally. There are a few signs that society is becoming more open about women's sexuality, but let us not get too excited about it. Over three decades after the 1970s trailblazers not only mentioned their vaginas, but they also looked at them, and most of them for the first time.

A cursory reading of the Australian Women's Weekly [AWW] up until the 1970s is amusing now, but not back then; women were subtly and overtly given the rules and dire warnings about the risks of the unknown – i.e., not observing the rules laid out in the articles and advice column in the AWW. The Weekly, as it was widely known, preached social certainties like, *a woman is never too young to know she has met the only man she will love*;[53] there were stories about men acting like wolves regarding women more as prey than partners. The story line only thinly covered the underlying warning for those who took a risk.[54] As late as 1963, the AWW's advice certainty was beginning to weaken. Take for instance, a tongue-in-cheek article about the power of a title for women doing domestic work. The heading *Time for housewives to get in the act* by upgrading titles from *cook* to *working housekeeper … kitchen maids* to *catering assistants* etc. One woman advised others to be on the safe side and stick to the title *Housewife* the next time it was necessary to describe your occupation.[55] The trail-blazing, NSW Women's Coordination Unit, led by the consummate femocrat, Helen L'Orange, in the early 1980s produced a clever booklet: *Occupation Housewife*, using the same notions.[56]

Then there's ageism and feeling invisible. No wonder those of us 70 and older feel we're becoming invisible, when women who reach 50 are beginning to feel the same; *the superficial, overt feeling of being invisible.*[57] A GP freelance writer, Evelyn Lewin, took up the issue on behalf of women several decades younger whose experiences are the subject of a book by broadcaster, writer and speaker, Jacinta Parsons.[58] And the source of their anger is *societal attitudes to ageing and invisibility women experience in midlife.* Sadly, Parsons herself appears to be captured by the very issue she is championing: the negative image of being older. Lewin quotes Parsons' observations about the jarring effect of *being seen as an older* woman.

For many, post-60 is when we confront both ageism and sexism. A 79-year-old health sociologist and freelance writer, Anne Ring, said, *don't dare call me young for my age.* She protested about phrases such as *youthful older adults* and *young at heart.* They are meant as compliments, but they are *assumptions based on negative images of what it is to be a woman over 70.*[59] In the same press, another young writer pointed out how the garment industry was ignoring young women who are over average size for their age: *Often in larger sizes, the clothes can be frumpy... but I don't want to look like I'm a grandma.*[60] As for me, I'm over 80, and for the life of me, I can't see why my age conjures only negative images. For me, and many like me, our lives continue to be as interesting and challenging as we want to make them. And that's what many of us are doing now we are free of the traditional caring role; we can choose how we spend our time and who we spend it with. The company of great-grandchildren is sheer joy. The 8th decade is not that different from the 6th or the 7th for that matter. A bit slower walking uphill, but many of us have more choices in our lives than in earlier times. And my sense of wellbeing is backed up by a research study showing women's *happiness levels tend to increase beyond midlife.*[61]

It might seem contradictory to be upset by negative images about our appearance while simultaneously protesting about becoming invisible. Think about it. These reactions do not cancel each other. What's more, both men and women feel invisible once they reach an age when they become *seniors.* A middle-aged woman seeing the inexorable march towards *invisibility* expressed her very strong feelings about the *astonishing power of this invisibility* in the title of her article, *Beware Invisible Angry Older Women: you won't see us coming.*[62] A social scientist, Dr Richard Hil, described his feelings sitting near a young couple who were recalling their acts of intimacy from the previous evening. Their disregard for his presence left Dr Hil feeling he might be invisible. His was not an isolated incident. A high-profile male television presenter, Richard Koch, was the recipient of what was excused as a misplaced joke when it masked ageist assumptions.[63] A young lawyer pointed out recently, *Many of us believe that being old means you're automatically incapable, unable, unfit.*[64] Another instance cropped up when the recent pandemic highlighted older people's discomfort. They reported feeling a sense of being invisible as all older people are grouped with a range of others in a category titled *vulnerable.* Disregarding older people was thus thoughtlessly reinforced by those managing the pandemic in Australia. The over-70s were grouped with the morbidly obese, those having treatment for terminal illnesses and other life-saving treatments. In circumstances like this, men, as well as women, experience a sense of being invisible.

For older women, the combination of entrenched sexism and ageism reinforces this sense of becoming invisible. In my experience, *it isn't the sexism we used to see in public life. Even though there's been legislation that should have eliminated it, it's something else I've felt happening for a while. I forget the actual situation that stopped me in my tracks when, for the first time, I realised I was no longer young.* This discussion has only just begun but I've concluded that people are far from getting the message. For instance, the former ABC program *The Drum*, which was very popular with older people - women in particular - rarely featured older presenters and subjects. We might also ask where is the literature dedicated to older women? This story will help stimulate others to fill the vacuum.

Chapter 6

How do older women live online?

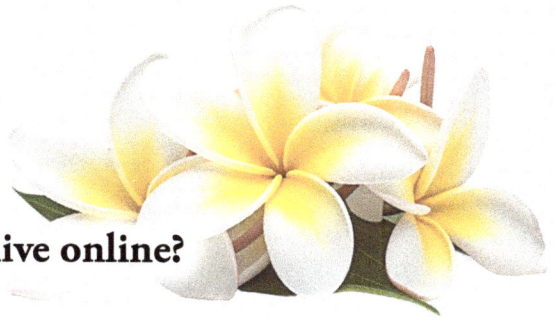

*We are a top-rated casual online sex site where men who
are curious about older women converge…*[65]

Annette

Don't give up your girlfriends or your vibrators.

Of course, you are good enough! He has a choice and will exercise it if he wants/needs to.I found it useful to apply what I called a *deficit model* to any man I met: everyone starts with 10/10 and as you get to know the person better, you can subtract points. Points cannot be regained or compensated for by something that you consider to be a plus. It's useful to bail out at about 7.5 out of 10.

When considering the possibility of sexual relations with a new man, be aware that many men of a *certain age* have problems in that department. It is useful to assume that they have a lowered level of testosterone, have had treatment for prostate cancer or similar, or suffer from *performance anxiety*. It is useful to assume that there will be no sex as you remember it, and then to consider if the man is still worth keeping company with for other reasons, and there might be a bonus in it for you if that's what you're looking for. I always *announced* that my orgasm was my responsibility, but that participation was welcomed. When he becomes irritating, think about your decision as being between him and a possible nothing, rather than between him and an improved version of him, because that possibility is unlikely. He ain't gonna change at this late stage! He has a whole life behind him, and you have a whole life behind you. What are the chances that those lives would dovetail? In your 70s and 80s avoid thinking about relationships and sex the way you did in the 1970s and 1980s.

Write your profile already, whether or not you ever use it online. It's like a CV for a job application. You become clear about who you are and what you are looking for in life.

***

How do older women live online? The short answer is most don't. Unlike me, many women beyond their 70s don't have a computer. These are the older people who are on the wrong side of the digital divide. But, for the adventurous minority who do venture online looking for company, there are guidelines and rules, and we can find them if we know where to look. How many of us know that Australia has an *e*Safety Commissioner[66] who has a check list to guide us through the minefield of options. I didn't. The determined will find it but what about the rest? Online is so accessible but is it safe? The experiences of a few of my friends are as alarming as they are informative.

Social life for older women quickly flags this question: do we have to change? When one friend turned up with an envelope and asked the only friend she knew well enough to mind the envelope in case she went missing, it started an adventure for both of them. One was stumbling into online dating. The other was freed to share her experience of dealing with loneliness in her marriage. The two friends, both over 70, did what no one else they knew did, they discussed their deeply felt need for intimacy and touch. In this very novel moment, they got down to discussing how it came about.

My contemporaries organised our husbands' social lives. And we know that it's safer for a single older male to go out at night than it is for a woman. Regardless of age, for that matter, being older simply adds more vulnerability. For instance, a man can drop into any bar, and most public bars and clubs, and usually continue to be included in suburban social gatherings. This is not the case for most women who are late 60s and older. While single older men are in great demand, very few older women say they are included in the social life of friends in couples. So, what do they do? We asked: *where do older women socialise to enjoy the company of others – men and women – who want to enjoy a connection with an other, not necessarily an other half?* We know fewer older men are around, especially from the mid to late 70s. But when one survives a partner, he has many more options than women the same age. He is in the minority for a start, so his eligibility far exceeds that of a single woman. But it's not confined to social life. In public life, not having a male, old or young, to act on her behalf, for instance, in buying or selling property, means an older woman is treated differently. Recent investigative programs have revealed that the isolation of older women targets them for scams – phone callers, posted mail, and especially online.

Culture changes, but do we? So why is this relevant to the sexuality of older women? Even women who'd become confident in their roles as change agents when young, now find populist political trends taking hold in democratic societies and effectively unwinding reforms women fought for and won last century. These are reforms like choices about health care and access to education and employment, to name a couple. Having won these reforms, older activists assumed they would be there for us as we age. It takes being on your own to bring into sharp focus the change that has happened in the last decade.

So where is this discussion starter going? It's one thing to acknowledge the physical effects of ageing on women's bodies, which is normal. What is not normal is the failure to recognise what continues regardless of growing older - our changing sense of ourselves. It's not so much a loss of what we've been through as a refreshed awareness of who we are and how we continue to see ourselves. Thus, the language used in public discourse - or missing from it - matters. Socialising on the internet is a whole new ball game. Even for women like me who've kept up with the technology, the internet is a new world. Keeping up with the technology is a technical skill but keeping up with the online society it has created is a whole new experience. Social life on the web is not bound by agreed rules or conventions, which takes us right back to the days of the wild west. It is a clear break from traditional rules and guidelines for social life and dating. For the uninitiated - which would include a substantial proportion of older women – it can be a minefield, as several of us found out. Based on their experiences, Ava and Annette have some interesting tips and sage advice.

NO drama, pretending, chasing, manipulating, agendas.

When I asked friends and acquaintances where they go to socialise, only those who used email mentioned the internet. For these women, the internet is largely a continuation of what they know – communicating with people they know. The ease means more contact, more often, regardless of age. We check email and social media more frequently than we ever checked our mailboxes, because notifications on our phones have a welcoming *ding* sound. Little wonder it soon feels very familiar. But only the brave searching for company tried online dating. It's a given; the internet has disrupted the way people communicate. It suits young people, the early adopters, and we now have an internet-based society. But, and there's always a but, it's wise to remember it's created mainly by young men who have grown up with technology. Many of us quickly learned how easy it is to use email. It's a permanent part of life even for those who do little else with the internet. In regional towns where social life can be pretty different from the city, there's one thing they have in common: the constraints and limitations on how and where older women can socialise casually. For Ava, meeting new people, especially men, reflects her professional life and frequent use of the internet. She urges women to bear the following in mind: *He has a whole life behind him, you have a whole life behind you, what are the chances that those lives would dovetail?*

So, what about socialising at home? I'd never lived alone until my partner of six decades died. And we are the generation who socialised at home - those 70's dinner parties were legendary at the time, and now are a distant history. But where else do the sexes gather to be with friends and possibly to meet new ones? I found the choice for older women is narrow indeed. But before we go any further, think about this reminder from Annette: *Don't believe your own negative assumptions e.g. that you'll never be invited to things if you don't have a partner. If you are unhappy alone, you will be unlikely to be invited to things!* And it's important because many women over 70 are living longer, healthier, and more active lives than their mothers' generation; at the same time there's the diminishing number of men of the same age range. Older women, partnered or alone, usually live among couples and families where women plan and organise entertainment. And entertainment is in the home—gatherings outside the family home stop with multi-generational picnics and the like. Single, older women don't fit this milieu. I won't go into it in this book, but where single older women live becomes increasingly significant for them when they want to continue as independent, socially active people.

What about trying dating apps? Those who looked at online dating sites will relate to the experiences of some older women I spoke to. I started this story because of what my inexperience taught me. Somewhat naively, I ventured onto a dating site and was stunned to find many so-called matches and expressions of interest from younger men, most of whom were very much younger. We have recently learned the whole so-called matching process is generated by AI [Artificial Intelligence]. I eventually learned that most are looking for free sex; for many, it's for sex only. In contrast, Ava's experience demonstrated something else: *I enrolled on a widely advertised and well-known site which was expensive, but I thought it would be safer and have a better chance of success as there is a comprehensive enrolment process.* She said, *I felt safe and took no risks…*because *they were all lovely men, and carefully screened.* Looking back on her experience, Ava concluded that *most of the men were lonely and interested in meeting a woman, but they had very little skill in moving forward. Some suffered guilt as they were widowers; wives mostly* *had died five or more years previously.* She had two experiences: *One man was lovely. We had a very enjoyable afternoon, but we agreed regrettably, there was no chemistry between us.* Ava did not give up, and then she met *Alex on another well-known site. We met, and we both had a sense of excitement and chemistry. He was almost too good to be true – therein lies a warning. We quickly moved into a sexual relationship which was wonderful for us both.* Sadly, months later and with no warning, Alex revealed *he felt the anxiety of commitment. He said that this was mostly his pattern, unable to commit. We ended the relationship.* Ava was understandably devastated. Sadly, her experience is not unusual.

In everyday life, we have a sort of gut reaction about who we can trust. With people, especially men we meet in our social network, we have the advantage of knowing a lot about them, how and where they live, and their family and friends. But how can we reassure ourselves online about the people we are meeting? When dating someone we know already in our network, we can usually predict how we will relate to one another. So, I asked my friends who've tried online dating about the difference when meeting someone from an unknown background. The virtual world has a lot of advantages and a lot of pitfalls. Not all are deliberate traps, but many are. Why? It comes down to why we are in this neutral space where we know nothing about each other. What is it we're looking for, and what do we expect? And this goes for the man we propose to meet as well as ourselves.

In all our relationships, trust and judgement are vital issues, but, online, there are *always* pitfalls, as Ava's experience demonstrated. Many older women on dating sites are surprised to be inundated with replies from younger males. Maybe the mistaken idea that older women lack choice and will take any male on offer is still out there. Generally, on most sites, but hidden in the settings or preferences section, there will be options to limit the age range of contacts and location – the nearer to where you live, the better. One friend, who had extensive public health experience and knew much about women's sexual behaviour and attitudes, shared what she had learned online. *The single older woman in affluent areas is seen as a honeypot, especially by younger, tech-savvy men. Older women who venture onto dating sites are seen as lonely and vulnerable, making them easy prey in the eyes of men. Not even ageing feminists share their inner lives, their sexual wants and needs, with each other.* It's kind of taboo for older women.

Online dating seems a good option for women who've kept up with technology. But everyone we spoke to agreed that it comes with many conditions and limitations. At the height of her professional life, Annette was very up to date with the internet and quickly learned how to use online dating sites. Her opening line of advice was: *Don't give up your girlfriends or your vibrators. I found it helpful to apply what I called a deficit model to any man I met: everyone starts with 10/10, and as you get to know the person better, you can subtract points. Points cannot be regained or compensated for by something you consider a plus. It's helpful to bail out at about 7.5 out of 10.* Annette, who had a professional career plus a good grip on sociological factors, including developing sexuality in young people, had a head start looking for a new partner in her later years.

Before you start out, you've gotta know what you want. As an SBS program *Asking for It* revealed, this is a huge issue.

Essentially, individuals of all ages and genders explained their experiences making their sexual wants known to a potential partner. What was especially striking for older women viewing this program was the confidence of individuals and their ease in expressing themselves. Neither the situation nor the opportunity to hear what others had to say existed until recent decades. Knowing what you want from other people is always good, but how many of us have asked ourselves this simple question? Several of my friends said they experienced something similar to mine: we were looking for companionship, someone to walk with, go to theatre and concerts with, and occasionally share a meal. Only a few reached the stage of putting their wants into action and dared to venture online. The savvy Annette already knew about essential safeguards, beginning with choosing a site. She learned to browse a range of sites and apps to decide on the best one for her. And she knew what she was looking for, as, in her retirement, she already had…*company, companions for outings, including walks and special events. There's always someone who shares my music and theatre,* she added. Annette's experience is an excellent guide to working out what's missing in your life, and what you're looking for.

It's also instructive to remind yourself about settling for less than you would have when you were young and were seeking a life partner. Why advice can make it safer. One of our contributors was advised by her friend, who knew much more about the habits of men who use online dating in Australia, to watch for the signs of scammers. Behaviour like being unavailable or uncontactable on weekends can indicate they are married and with their family. And many people tell lies especially on dating apps. Another safeguard is staying close to home, which should increase the likelihood of similar backgrounds and circumstances, e.g., education, tastes, housing and income. Too often, people evaluate women for their assets rather than their social needs. One contact made it clear she wanted daytime meetings only.

There are numerous guides to help ensure the safe use of apps and dating sites, including that of the *e*Safety Commissioner, which stresses the importance of understanding how your devices work and, even more critical, how scammers operate. Lastly, of course, is understanding your own behaviour.

Jane gave us the following tips for keeping your life private, at least initially. Always avoid using your real first name; and while you should use photos of yourself on the dating site, use only ones taken explicitly for use on a dating site, instead of the ones you might use on social media etc. An internet image search can produce many hits and could help name and localise you. Remember, internet image search works both ways - you search your potential partner's profile photos. You might be surprised at what you find. Then, creating a dating email address can be helpful. Use that one to register on the dating site to swap emails with a potential contact if necessary. It also means your regular email address doesn't get dating spam.

Take your time, don't be in too much of a hurry is another good rule. Thinking back about her experience, Margot urged older women to: *Pause and think how you'd explain to your friends and family that you met a man on the net. Keep this in mind, and you're on your way to understanding survival guidelines.* We asked what taking time to get to know a man you've met on a dating site meant. One woman's response summed up the experience of several: *If you've felt the hollowness of being alone, of not having a partner you feel connected to, that's when you're likely to forget being cautious. And even if you think about where this man might have been, who he'd have been with, can you believe him? When he doesn't want to use a condom and says it spoils his pleasure, what then?* As far as becoming sexual in the online dating world, it's here that caution is critical. And it comes down to a set of steps. It's a matter of how to take the time to get to know someone you've only met on the net. We usually find that in a face-to-face meeting, we can make a more precise assessment of the person than we can online, no matter how many photographs and messages we exchange.

Do online relationships last? It's a fair question, and so is a very apt quote which sums up the motivation for many older women: *I want to be cared for before I'm in a care home and looked after before I need to be.* The experiences of women I know - admittedly a tiny sample - are worth sharing because they seem so normal; they are not usually shared or written down where others could find them. For starters, they all experienced the pleasure of flirting just as they had in their youth. It's the essence of a virtual relationship that works. And we've read how virtual relationships develop much faster than in-person ones, but usually end much earlier. It must be stressed that this applies to people who meet for the first time online.

In contrast to the experience of people who meet for the first time online, there is evidence that relationships that endure are between people who've known each other for some time. In one sense, it's not surprising. Both parties already know a lot about each other, how they've lived, family and past relationships, and many personal traits, including humour. Marion told me how she and her lover progressed, from *innocent messaging to explicit longing. From expressing inner feelings to secret desires when we formed a friendship, we had known each other for many years. It happened by chance. From the beginning, we kept to the reason we had made contact. Then, after some time, a chance comment sparked a new direction.* They had always found each other attractive, but it took a significant change in circumstances in both their lives before a chance meeting not only brought them together but sparked renewed interest in each other. With background knowledge of the person, a virtual relationship allows both parties to be different, even braver than they might be in person, about their wants and needs in a partner. Greetings like; *Good morning, precious,* or partings which include *I'll wait for your touch,* are easier to exchange in print than in person. One woman told us how she re-read his messages which thrilled her each time.

That first meeting, appearance and first sexual encounter are worth mentioning here. For women of any age, the usual expectation involves appearance, especially our own. But it's different for most men. While I fretted about my appearance, I was reassured when he described his expectation, *oh, she's taking her clothes off for me.* As far as we know, these different expectations are not unique to our immediate networks. Most advice regarding setting up the first and subsequent meetings stresses the importance of meeting in a neutral place. And, importantly, make sure a trusted friend has the details of your plans. These are all necessary safeguards. Apart from journalists and artists, few women have much experience describing themselves. The women I spoke to had difficulty writing a profile, describing themselves and what they are looking for, and even what their opening words might be. It might be tempting to use an older photo, but remember, if a meeting occurs, only an up to date one will do. Importantly, before meeting a person you don't know, male or female, it is wise to provide the details to someone you trust in the event you come to harm.

Do we need to care about safe sex? Well, all guidelines and individual experiences emphasise one point: don't wade in without knowing what you are doing. There are official government websites, but for our sample group, none of them knew about the Australian *e*Safety Commissioner's site and its guidelines. We know that age does not protect you from sexually transmitted diseases. Nursing staff are increasingly worried that sex is now permitted, if not encouraged, among residents in aged care. Consequently, the risk of diseases such as syphilis, gonorrhoea, chlamydial infection, genital herpes, hepatitis and genital warts is becoming more prevalent in older generations.[67] Almost everyone who is sexually active also runs the risk of being infected with *HIV*. Unprotected sex is quite common among the older generation. These diseases were not a worry to them in their youth, and now in their older age, they also enjoy the freedom of not worrying about pregnancy. Generally, men prefer unprotected sex because wearing a condom reduces sensation and exacerbates *ED* issues. Some women also prefer unprotected sex because using a condom reduces their sensation. The wise advice is: *If it's not on, it's not on,* but the decision must be mutual. It is something that must be discussed. It may be embarrassing at the time, but it will not be as embarrassing as explaining the medication you take to your children later, or why you need a lift to the hospital sexual health clinic.

What's it like online; in other words, doing it virtually? The distance in time and space in the online world makes everything possible. I admit I knew next to nothing about using a dating site. In ignorance, I assumed it worked the same way I'd experienced face-to-face meetings in my life. I've bought and sold property and travelled alone in other countries – even places where I didn't speak the language. I knew how to meet with my kids' teachers. I even knew my MP. Notably, I also knew how and where I could learn about them. For me, the virtual was not only a whole new experience. It allowed me time to think about what I wanted to say and even say things I would be hesitant to speak about in person. This could explain how virtual relationships grow and blossom faster than face-to-face ones.

Annette, who had a professional background, knew the ground rules before she entered the online dating world. She had all the safeguards in place, and, over time, she amended the process of what to expect and what adjustments to previous relationship experiences were necessary. And she developed her evaluation standards, including a *deficit* model, reminding herself that sex life in later decades will not be a repeat of younger ones. These rules and safeguards are much harder to apply on the net, particularly for older women who did not grow up with this exciting technology.

Whatever gets you through the night seems a trite conclusion. But it applies more often than we think. For many women and men, sleeping problems come with ageing – getting off to sleep, staying asleep and getting back to sleep after waking during the night. Medical professionals often speak of the importance of sleep to health and wellbeing, especially for our brains. We can feel the tension in muscles and aching joints and can take medication for this. But it's so much harder to control our mental state. Several women told me about waking in the night and resorting to using a vibrator, often referred to as a sex toy. That and manual masturbation. Marion told me about her experience: *I'm still getting used to living on my own and find it hard to get back to sleep when I wake in the night. I start going over a few things if I've had a busy day. I don't know where I read it, but someone wrote about using a vibrator – clitoral stimulation is a good distraction! I use it from time to time, and it does help me relax and get back to sleep.* I wondered whether a device such as a vibrator is ever recommended to older women instead of medication. Sometimes hot milk is just not enough. But, again, this seems to be an area where more open discussion could be helpful in the way it was for my contributors.

Maybe a little sexual diversion is as good a sleep inducer as any pill the doctor can provide.

Chapter 7

Older, but not out

I never miss a chance to have sex or appear on television.
Gore Vidal[68]

Margot

Ageing bodies complicate sex for our age group – hips are a big problem for intercourse. Trying out different positions is all well and good but by the time we have got ourselves into position, it is hard to maintain an erection or lubrication or desire with all the experimenting. Malcolm has a very high bed – I need a stool to get onto it – and we found that the most comfortable position for intercourse was for him to stand beside the bed and for me to be on the very edge. However, he needs to wear shoes that will not slip on the carpet! I also find that I need copious amounts of KY jelly to ensure that I am properly lubricated. Sexual desire and activity can be affected by other things like our digestive systems – have we had a large meal; do we have reflux or indigestion; are our bowels working okay; are we tired? We shower together and cuddle a lot. We hold hands and kiss often. We laugh a lot in bed and try to make sex playful. I often wonder about how those men who are completely penetration focused are coping in old age with failing orgasms and erections.

I have been completely gobsmacked by this turn of events. It has been 40 years since my marriage ended, and I certainly wasn't expecting in old age to meet this wonderful man after all those years of being unsuccessful in my attempts to meet a new partner. However, years of independence have made it difficult for me to return to a traditional live-in relationship.

Sophie

It might be how we relate to attractive people - or just like a lot. For me, it has always been about the other person, as that is how my husband and I worked out our sex life. There wasn't much information to guide us, but we knew what pleased each other. For my husband, it was knowing we'd be having sex the following day – mornings were best for both of us, even when we were young. I think I was fairly inhibited –that's how I would describe myself after reading about many other women's reactions. I might even be more open to ideas and experimentation later than when I was young.

I know this is not unusual, but I've had the chance to experience the pleasure of a new relationship. What really surprised me was the excitement and sexual arousal, just like when I was young. So, I thought, well, some things don't change as we get older despite the way most women are seen once they get beyond their 70s. Added to the excitement is knowing what I am doing. Better late than never!

Julie Bates, a senior sex worker

I am still working, but today I see myself as a caregiver of sorts in the world's oldest profession. My first visit with a client in a nursing home some years ago was when a woman contacted me to visit her then 90-year-old father. As I usually do before I see a client, I find out a little about them. Knowing as I do, it's as much about having a person there all to themselves as it is about sex. It is good to share a conversation on a subject they are familiar with, and even a tipple of their choice. On one occasion, I learned my client was a well-known and respected pianist who loved a glass of sherry. On that day, his daughter left two little old-fashioned sherry glasses on the bench and a bottle of sherry in the fridge. He and I shared a glass of sherry and a chat, and the rest, of course, is personal between him and me!

***

Even now, imagine if an older woman said what Gore Vidal did decades ago. Our leaders need to heed what older people have been saying for some time, about where they prefer to live and where they prefer to die. The figure has varied from between 70-80% on whether they wish to die at home or in a hospital. Sadly, the reverse is consistently true. It takes determined effort to act alone and prepare for dying at home as our health system is focused on two goals: keeping people alive as long as possible and preventing access to medicine or means which enable people to die at home. But this topic deserves a study on its own. For now, my focus is on the existing system and noting behaviour such as the decision to move into residential care; it happens for a range of reasons. Older people needing to be cared for could result from something as simple as loss of mobility due to a broken leg which is slow to recover. For older people who live alone, injury can make residential care the only option. Some freely choose it in preference to be managing a free-standing building. For everyone, it's a whole new experience and while there are other people close by, it is still solo living. Outwardly, this situation should increase the opportunity for finding a like-minded friend, but few are as lucky as Margot was when she met a like-minded man. – they bonded over a cause they were both passionate about – and recently *celebrated the anniversary of our meeting, which only happened because we both attended a course about climate change. We quickly discovered during the tea break that we had a lot of shared values, and he asked me to join him for lunch. I was astounded to be asked out on a date – it was so long since I had even thought about the possibility.*

Many others simply continue to miss having an other half. You know the scene: you see or read something which stirs feelings that you have not given any, or much, thought to before. Then you turn to your partner, and, without much introduction, you begin to speak what's in your mind. It's hard to replace that loss amongst the many ongoing yearnings for what has been lost. As Julie Bates, who works in aged care and told me how a relative asked her to help her 90-year-old father, who wished for some company. She paints an enchanting picture of her and her client enjoying a glass of sherry provided by his daughter. What happened after is between her and the man but whatever did occur, it is important to note that it was with the approval of the nursing home and his relatives. Her experience is, *while it's good to be able to converse on a subject they are familiar with…it's as much about having a person there all to themself as it is about sex.* Julie is not a nurse, a doctor or a care assistant; she is a sex worker. It may surprise many people, but it is becoming mainstream now for her to work with residents in some nursing homes. Julie said, *there are nursing care plans in place for guidance during visits from sexual partners, including sex workers. The nursing staff are encouraging.* Margot commented on the pleasure and *intimacy of lying naked together*, a joy denied older people who must live in shared spaces.

A worker with experience caring for older people, said that older people she knew… *never stop feeling.*[69] But the story about the overpowering needs that older people have for closeness and touch should not have been surprising. While ever no one is asking older people about their need for an intimate other, the mere thought of older people continuing to enjoy having sex, gets headlines for its novelty value only. For instance, a story about a couple – he's 100 and she's 96 – finding love and romance with each other made the news for no other reason than the age of the people.[70] But it promises there is hope for the future. If we think of older people being sexual, we can talk about it too. Sex in shared homes is something everyone should be able to talk about because the subject is not going away, and someday, we or our children will have to address it. A 78-year-old man got a half page in the SMH with the attention-grabbing headline: *I've stopped sleeping with my wife. Now we really sleep.*[71] He makes a good point about couples having different sleep patterns and, apart from the cheeky statement …*all children know that their parents stop having sex once they are over 70*, the focus of the article is on where they sleep. He noted teasingly, that *maintaining the relationship and intimacy that normally comes from sleeping together*, we are left to wonder whether his wife might be as satisfied as he clearly is. There has been nothing comparable from an older woman, married or single.

Adult children and the sexual life of their parents is an age-old issue. They don't like discussing sex and their parents in the same sentence. It's an age-old situation: adult children do not see their parents as sexual beings. They don't want to. In my sample of women friends, it's not ceasing to desire shared intimacy, it's about finding a partner to share it with. Very few are as lucky as Margot or Sophie. And the family who engaged Julie Bates for her relative in aged care is the exception rather than the rule.

The French have always had a different approach to sexual behaviour regardless of age. It is really one of the essentials of life no matter how it is practised. According to Marie de Hennezel in her book, *Sex after Sixty*,[72] intimacy is important in maintaining a sex life as we age. She includes a quote from Anais Nin: *The only magic against death, ageing, ordinary life, is love.*

Once we accept that older people continue to be sexual beings, we understand something else. That is, older people still have a sex life as a panellist, 71 year old Gwenda Darling, told a Sydney conference recently. Gwenda was diagnosed with frontotemporal dementia in 2011.[73] Along with the example of 80-year-old Stephanie Alexander about the quality of life which includes an intimate other, there's the experiences of myself and my older women friends. We await the interest of serious social policy research so we can add our lived experiences to those of other older people who, like us, continue to want the pleasure of shared intimacy.

CONCLUSION

…we were the era of free love…I think we would still be engaging in sexual relationships as we did 50, 60 years ago if we weren't stopped.[74]

The words of Gwenda Darling should not be the clarion call to families and carers that they are. Older people continue to be sexual beings and a dementia diagnosis does not automatically mean that a person lacks the capacity to consent to a relationship.[75] We got on with it when we were young; we got on with it in the 1970s; and we are still being asked to just get on with it. Get on with what? Ask an older woman who finds herself living alone if she misses anything. It won't take long to learn that for many, it's the comforting touch of an other half. Should you go further and ask whether she still wants the pleasure of an intimate partner, you could be in for another surprise. Why all the surprises? Why indeed.

Waking up in an octogenarian body is the story I set out to share. I began my investigation tentatively at first but eventually accepting that solo living is here to stay after my partner of 60 years died. Gone was the pleasure of a shared life - shared experiences, shared conversations and a shared bed. Sharing the big things and the seemingly casual, like the pat as he said *goodnight darling*, or the casual comment like, *I always enjoy watching you undress.* Part of the new beginning was wondering how others, ordinary women like me had coped. It was then that I shared my question with a friend: *is this all there is to life?* I soon learned I am not alone, and the stories of very separate journeys came tumbling out. Ten older women share not only their lived experience after their partnered lives ended, but they also shared a lot more. And their experiences encompass so much of what it is to be a typical older woman now.

We live in a time when feelings are the subject of conversations – in person, in groups, in meetings, and online – but not if the feelings are those of older women. I've dug down to ask why but, also how, we gradually became invisible, lost to public view or even concern. It's a story of how language is used to shape thought and persuade society to a viewpoint without ever involving the people concerned, women who are in their 70s, 80s and beyond. It includes the era of social revolution when the current generation of older women were at the forefront of change in the 1970s. These same women were children when it was commonly believed that children should be *seen and not heard.*

As today's older women transitioned from childhood to being recognised as an adult on their 21st birthday, they did not experience what is common today, the identity which came with being an adolescent. Advertising discovered that cohort when they started earning money. Fortunately for them, the adolescent experience is now recognised if not always understood and respected. While being an older woman continues to be little known beyond individual experience.

This conversation starter should stimulate discussion and, eventually lead to a time when being older is not only recognised it is respected for what we bring to society. Or can bring, if only we are asked. It's yet another taboo to be broken open.

But first, thorough research into the lived experience of older women has to be collected, analysed and shared. Only then will stereotypes be replaced by real people, our real-life experiences, variations and helpful advice.

APPENDIX 1
Friends' experiences of 'getting on with it'

[Not their real names to protect their privacy]

Annette

Don't give up your girlfriends or your vibrators.

- Of course, you are good enough! He has a choice and will exercise it if he wants/needs to.

- I found it useful to apply what I called a *deficit model* to any man I met: everyone starts with 10/10 and as you get to know the person better you can subtract points. Points cannot be regained or compensated for by something that you consider to be a plus. It's useful to bail out at about 7.5 out of 10.

- When considering the possibility of sexual relations with a new man, be aware that many men of a *certain age* have problems in that department. It is useful to assume that they have a lowered level of testosterone, have had treatment for prostate cancer or similar, or suffer from *performance anxiety*. It is useful to assume that there will be no sex as you remember it, and then to consider if the man is still worth keeping company with for other reasons, and there might be a bonus in it for you if that's what you're looking for. I always *announced* that my orgasm was my responsibility, but that participation was welcomed.

- When he becomes irritating, think about your decision as being between him and a possible "nothing", rather than between him and an improved version of him, because that possibility is unlikely. He ain't gonna change at this late stage!

- He has a whole life behind him, and you have a whole life behind you. What are the chances that those lives would dovetail?

- In your 70s and 80s avoid thinking about relationships and sex the way you did in the 1970s and 1980s.

- Write your profile already, whether or not you ever use it online. It's like a CV for a job application. You become clear about who you are and what you are looking for in life.

- Look for signs of *courting behaviour* from a man but be careful that it is not "love bombing".

- Don't believe your own negative assumptions e.g. that you'll never be invited to things if you don't have a partner. If you are unhappy alone, you will unlikely be invited to things!

- Do you find him boring? Men communicate very differently to women. They can do a lot of talking that has nothing to do with you. Perhaps find ways of dealing with the fact that he is unlikely to change and don't give up on your girlfriends!

- How to deal with their exes: exorcise them! Why would you need to know about them? Be aware that there are many different marital states: widowed; divorced; never married; separated; looking for a wife.

- When putting yourself *out there* it is much better to present a good version of yourself than a fantastic version of *someone else* who you imagine might be more appealing than you. Remember women tend to dress for other women and men are often oblivious to the way women look except in a general sense. I loved the slogan stuck on the mirror in the fitting room in a Green Point dress shop: *my darling your arms look FINE!* (@sister bojangles).

NO drama, pretending, chasing, manipulating agendas.

Ava

I enrolled on a widely advertised and well-known site which was expensive, but I thought it would be safer and have a better chance of success as there is a comprehensive enrolment process. I met 5 or 6 men over a one-year period. They were all lovely men and carefully screened. I felt safe and took no risks.

Most of the men were lonely and interested in meeting a woman, but they had very little skill in moving forward. Some suffered guilt as they were widowers; wives mostly had died five or more years previously. Some had created busy lives around giving service to adult families and grandchildren. A couple had created lives around a good cause.

One man was lovely. We had a very enjoyable afternoon, but we agreed regrettably, there was no chemistry between us.

I met Alex on another well-known site, he replied to my initial entry in minutes. We met, we both had a sense of excitement and chemistry. He was almost too good to be true – therein lies a warning. We quickly moved into a sexual relationship which was wonderful for us both. Four to five months later he had a panic attack and bailed out; he felt *anxiety of commitment*. He said that this was mostly his pattern, unable to commit. We ended the relationship.

I was shattered, I went into a classic grief response, which stunned my family, who remained mostly silent and watched me carefully.

I think life-long monogamy is not realistic. I would consider a relationship with a married man. I have flirted with two married men, but not taken it any further.

Brigit

Alone at home after the death of your partner. It's confronting to think about it and it's very confronting when it happens. I was only 43 when my husband died very suddenly in an accident, leaving me with small children to raise alone.

So how did I cope then? Slowly, over some years, I came to realise that there's a difference between being alone, and the deep loneliness stemming from the lack of intimacy.

Everybody will have different coping strategies for not being alone… putting the radio on to fill the deafening stillness of an empty house, phoning friends, creating a new routine of life and melding an old one into it. It takes continued effort to take such agency in a time of stunned listlessness but it's necessary if you don't want to be alone. Others remember you are on your own for a while but then they expect you to manage your own life again… by yourself.

Coping with that deep loneliness and lack if intimacy is another matter and I would say it's very individual. It takes time to be able to emotionally accept that your former relationship is physically over and can never return. It takes time to not feel guilty about wanting to be held. It takes time to understand that the heart has many rooms and that your partner will always be in his no matter how many other doors you open.

About four years after my husband died, I went back to the sailing club we had been members of. In that easy environment I learned to be in the company of men again and to feel single. I had a few fun but not lasting relationships. It took courage to allow myself to be held and to be sexual again, and the relationships wouldn't have started if I had not felt more confident of myself as a separate person. The age of internet dating had not begun so I did not have that means of meeting men so my interest groups were my social outlet, when my family duties permitted.

I married again when I was sixty, to a man who introduced himself to me at a rugby match which I was reluctantly attending with my family. My second marriage is different from my first. I am different now, more self-sufficient emotionally and physically. He is a different person. We share a different phase of life. He has a terminal illness so I may well outlive him and be on my own again.

So yes, that still is a confronting thought, but I now know only I can create the life I want to have. Only I can seek out people and draw them closer to me if I want company and that to soften that other deep and natural longing for close intimacy with another partner I first have to be OK being my own good.

Margot

Last week Malcolm and I celebrated the anniversary of our meeting, which only happened because we both attended a course about climate change. We quickly discovered during the tea break that we had a lot of shared values, and he asked me to join him for lunch. I was astounded to be asked out on a date – it was so long since I had even thought about the possibility.

In brief, my husband was my first boyfriend at 21, and we married within a year of meeting. My sexuality was robust, and I loved sex, and he and I learned a lot about sex by reading *Forum* magazines. The full-time, stay-at-home mother role did not fulfil me; I was lonely and felt like I was going mad. That's when I discovered the Women's Electoral Lobby (WEL) and met women who have continued as dear friends. A high point was the mid-decade UN Conference on women. I embraced women talking about politics and women's rights. After I read *The Feminine Mystique* (by Betty Friedan), I joined a group of women seeking to further their education. Alas, it was the beginning of the end of my marriage. I totally missed all the cues about how unhappy he was until one day he came home from work and said he was leaving. We did try marriage guidance counselling, but his heart wasn't in it – he left and the next day moved in with a woman with whom he was working. Our children were 9 and 7, and I was devastated and on the brink of giving up university, but the other women – all mature-aged students – convinced me to keep studying.

I'd had a satisfying and enjoyable sex life in marriage, and I felt bereft and completely rejected. I did note that the marriage break-up rate of mature-age women students at Macquarie University was running at about 50%. I knew I was not alone in coordinating shared parenting and study. With a few of the women I'd met, we visited bars and various dating sites. I was keen to try these new venues but was disappointed. In the workforce after graduation, I attracted the attention of a lot of married men. I wasn't flirting with them, but they must have seen my longing for intimacy. I'm not proud of these liaisons, which I always saw as convenient for both parties. They were intelligent me; I had evenings out, good conversations and sex which satisfied us both. It was part of life working for Canberra MPs. But it seemed almost impossible for me to meet single men with whom I had a rapport and shared   philosophies.

Eventually, my self-esteem improved as I became more successful in my jobs; after menopause, the urge for sex didn't seem so strong. Then again, I always had a vibrator. Working for the Family Planning organisation improved my confidence in my sexuality and self-esteem. I discovered interesting erotic books. Right up until the last job before I retired, I was still having a go with trying to find someone through internet dating and it was just as hopeless as it had always been. At one time I tried to do a count in my head of all the men I had had sex with since my divorce, and the number shocked me. I had a lot of one-night stands. One of the things I did learn from such a large sample size was that there were very few men who were any good at sex that suited me. I have never had an orgasm with straight intercourse, and I have had successful sex (from my point of view) with only 5 men.

As a carer, I gave up even thinking about finding a partner. Now, I'm in a village community. I decided I wouldn't have a relationship with a married man and certainly wouldn't contemplate taking on someone who was just looking for a housekeeper/nurse in their dotage. I met a great group of women through the University of the Third Age, and I had given up any thoughts of having a late-life relationship. After my carer role ended (my mum died) it occurred to me one day that I was the happiest and most content that I had ever been in my life. However, I still reached for my vibrator and erotic books occasionally.

Then I met Malcolm. He'd been married happily for over 45 years. He'd tried internet dating after his wife died. He also read books about sex and internet dating. He was enjoying cycling and had given up actively looking for a partner. Malcolm is 80 and has health problems endemic to men of his age. When we first met, he had to go into hospital for erectile dysfunction (ED) and his urologist prescribed an injection. It helps him to get an erection but it's difficult to maintain – he didn't find Viagra useful.

Together we visited the local sex shop – it's part of a chain that is owned by a woman and run by women who all know the products and what they can do. We purchased a cock ring and that, combined with the injection, enables him to have a good erection that lasts for probably 20-30 minutes. I was happy to find that Malcolm is one of those rare men that can give me an orgasm (without intercourse). He knows about a woman's clitoris, where it is and what to do with it. He explained that he'd read about it. At the beginning of our relationship, my dormant sexuality suddenly went ballistic and my whole body was in a constant state of sexual excitement for a few months which was amazing. I hadn't had so many orgasms since I was first married. Thank goodness it has settled down a lot after 12 months of us sleeping together.

At our age, we've learnt that sex is very different from when we were younger. Although Malcolm has been able to have and maintain an erection with the aid of the injection and cock ring, he has not had an orgasm since we met. This has worried me a bit because it seems that I am getting all the pleasure. He seems sanguine about it because of what he has read about the problems of sex for older men, but he does still enjoy the feeling of intercourse with me. He says he also gets great pleasure from my orgasms and the intimacy of lying naked together and feeling my breasts on his chest.

Ageing bodies complicate sex for our age group – hips are a big problem for intercourse. Trying out different positions is all well and good but by the time we have got ourselves into position, it is hard to maintain an erection or lubrication or desire with all the experimenting. Malcolm has a very high bed – I need a stool to get onto it – and we found that the most comfortable position for intercourse was for him to stand beside the bed and for me to be on the very edge. However, he needs to wear shoes that will not slip on the carpet! I also find that I need copious amounts of KY jelly to ensure that I am properly lubricated. Sexual desire and activity can be affected by other things like our digestive systems – have we had a large meal; do we have reflux or indigestion; are our bowels working okay; are we tired? We shower together and cuddle a lot. We hold hands and kiss often. We laugh a lot in bed and try to make sex playful. I often wonder about how those men who are completely penetration focused are coping in old age with failing orgasms and erections.

I have been completely gobsmacked by this turn of events. It has been 40 years since my marriage ended and I certainly wasn't expecting in old age to meet this wonderful man after all those years of being unsuccessful in my attempts to meet a new partner. However, years of independence have made it difficult for me to return to a traditional live-in relationship. Malcolm has his set routines and habits, and I have mine and it is quite difficult fitting into someone else's timetables and at times, things can get a bit tetchy. We have been working on how to best manage our relationship and it has changed a couple of times since we became serious about one another. We spend four nights together at his place – it's bigger than my place – and then I have three nights at home alone. On the four nights we spend together we take turns with the cooking and cleaning up. Even when we have nights apart, we still often do things together during the day, like bush walking, going to the movies, or having lunch out. We each have a spare bedroom which I often use because I am a terrible sleeper. However, I feel amazed that we share so much in common. Malcolm has no problems at all about my feminism and independence. We agree on politics and concern for the environment, and we love classical music, live theatre, films, bush walking, art, photography and are in awe of nature. In addition, Malcolm is a very principled and nice man and so all these things in common help us to overcome any difficulties experienced in bed and lead to a wonderful intimate relationship.

I took HRT for many years, prescribed by a Chinese doctor and made up at a compounding pharmacy until such time as the doctor thought I was becoming too old to keep taking it! I've found *Vagifem* helps with stress incontinence, and I continue to use it. Anxiety about bladder leakage and irritable bowel syndrome problems led me to have a bidet toilet seat installed in my bathroom. When I started spending the night with Malcolm, he also had one installed at his place.

I am quite uninhibited with sex and seem to have the knack of making it fun. Malcolm told me he had not laughed so much in bed with women from other relationships. It's part of our enjoyable sex life.

Marion

I am very interested in how other women my age – I'm in my early 80s – continue to want the pleasure I've always had with sex. I have my share of health problems. And I'm keen to follow the rules for getting the most out of life – exercising, eating good food and having an interest that keeps my brain ticking over. It's hard to pick up a newspaper without finding an article that goes over this advice to older people. But I've noticed there is never much talk about our sex lives – none really.

So, when the very unexpected happened, having a sexual encounter in my 80s, I was very excited. After all, I was getting used to being *old*, and, like everyone else, I'd accepted that there wasn't much left to find out, especially about myself. There was no one I could talk to now that I'm alone. I never thought I would write about it. But I can say that my body is very alive to my new partner. We meet infrequently as it's what we call an *illicit* relationship – I think that adds to the pleasure.

I'm still getting used to living on my own and find it hard to get back to sleep when I wake in the night. I start going over a few things if I've had a busy day. I don't know where I read it, but someone wrote about using a vibrator – clitoral stimulation is a good distraction! I've only tried it a couple of times, but it does help me relax and get back to sleep.

I'm grateful to you for talking about something which matters a lot to me. I wonder if my experience is not so rare, as there aren't many possible partners for women my age.

Sophie

I'm a leftover of the 1970s in more ways than one. I met up with women my age, and they seemed to know the main problems for women. And they had good ideas about how to tackle them. That's how I got into community life as a stay-at-home wife and mother. So many of us still were back then. But now we look back and are proud of the changes our generation made.

I know I am one of the lucky ones, as my husband and I had a good life and relationship. It was so good we even had a daring adventure and came through it in one piece! It was very much part of the era of change. My husband and I had a short-term experience with partner exchange. I look back on this now and am amused by how it was described: wife swapping.

And it engages me as, in our case, the *wife-swapping* was driven by the wife of the other couple.

I was the last to realise what was happening – she was that kind of self-confident woman. The other man and I were not carried away by it. We enjoyed it at the time. It began suddenly, and my reaction may seem odd nowadays. One evening I found myself alone in the lounge room. Everyone had disappeared. I waited a while and then went to bed. Then my bedroom door opened, and the other man came in and began removing his clothes. I realised the conversation we'd had earlier about flirtatious behaviour must have meant something. It had involved the usual sexual innuendo, including how pleased he was by large breasts like mine. It was both a surprise and not a surprise when he immediately began kissing and squeezing my breasts. My husband and I learned later this behaviour was not a novel experience for them.

My reaction was mainly about the excitement of doing something like this with my husband's approval. Although I realised that there was a strong sexual attraction between my husband and the woman, even so, perhaps foolishly, I never felt our relationship was under threat. I always felt secure in our relationship, and it never crossed my mind that my husband would leave me. It Seems odd now as I look back on this experience.

I can't say I have any advice or tips to pass on to other women about having a good sexual relationship. It might be how we relate to attractive people - or just like a lot. For me, it has always been about the other person, as that is how my husband and I worked out our sex life. There wasn't much information to guide us, but we knew what pleased each other. For my husband, it was knowing we'd be having sex the following day – mornings were best for both of us, even when we were young. It continued that way throughout our long partnership. I think I was fairly inhibited –that's how I would describe myself after reading about many other women's reactions. I might even be more open to ideas and experimentation later than when I was young. Luckily, I've found this out, and a late-blooming love affair has challenged me enough to speak to others I know about our relationship for the first time.

I know this is not unusual, but I've had the chance to experience the pleasure of a new relationship. What really surprised me was the excitement and sexual arousal, just like when I was young. So, I thought, well, some things don't change as we get older despite the way most women are seen once they get beyond their 70s. Added to the excitement is knowing what I am doing. Better late than never!

Julie Bates OA - *a senior sex worker*
I am still working but today I see myself as a caregiver of sorts in the world's oldest profession.

My first visit with a client in a nursing home some years ago was when a woman contacted me to visit her then 90-year-old father. As I usually do before I see a client, I find out a little about them. Knowing as I do, it's as much about having a person there all to themselves as it is about sex, it is good to be able to share a conversation on a subject they are familiar with, and even a tipple of their choice. On this particular occasion I learnt my client was a well-known and respected pianist and loved a glass of sherry.

On that day, his daughter left two little old fashioned sherry glasses on the bench and a bottle of sherry in the fridge. He and I shared a glass of sherry and a chat and the rest of course, is personal between him and I!

Another client I recall, where I had to dig deep into my bag of skills, was with a young man who had been involved in a serious car accident and had become a paraplegic. He had lost all sensation from just below his nipples but we found a way for him to have some pleasure. His mates brought him to me, and whilst I was with the young man, they sat patiently waiting for him outside. They even coughed up when he wanted to extend our session. It was a real gesture of friendship – that they could do this for him.

APPENDIX 2

Women's Electoral Lobby – office politics

Asmall but eager group of volunteers gathered in the Grosvenor Street WEL office in the early 1980s; most of us yet to take our place in the paid workforce. At the height of our activism, we were all busy caring for our families, and some were continuing with study programs. The office was made available to us by a generous benefactor, Stella Cornelius, a noted businesswoman at the time. We all worked as many hours as we could manage on two to three days a week. Pam Simons worked all the time, at home, on holidays, when she woke in the evenings. She was a mainstay. We gathered stories from individuals to build case studies and, with a bit of help, wrote legislation to put our case to government as we appealed for support.

The era of dramatic changes, brought about by the social upheaval of the 1970s in NSW, is part of the story of The Women's Electoral Lobby [WEL]. Its proponents, its defenders, and, ultimately, the community of women which developed in relatively few years, were at the heart of many changes; and, in some significant areas, WEL was a leader of the change. Thanks to the epoch-making reforms of the Whitlam government, many of us were mature age students in higher education through 1970s and 80s. We gained skills and formed many new friendships which continued for the remainder of our lives.

It was all pre word processing machines, mobile phones, and office fax machines. Slowly we acquired equipment –

usually when someone knew someone whose office was being upgraded. All communication involved letters, envelopes, stamps and delivery to the post office. Lists of MPs for instance, had to be drawn up by hand. There was a lot of pitching in to help. We thought we were made when someone picked up a second-hand electric typewriter – it had 35-character memory. But it was a revolution in the WEL office.

Previously, meeting deadlines with documents on the old iron typewriter – all foolscap paper, carbon copies – tested our skills. Meeting the deadline for the submission for the initial OH&S for women in paid workforce was memorable. The Premier, Hon Neville Wran, responded to the request [WEL's included] and submissions were called for. The senior bureaucrat at the time was not a supporter but, fortunately, Wran's support prevailed. However, it meant that there was a very short time frame for submissions to be lodged. We in the WEL office had to gather the data from industry, government departments, universities, and to our relief, everyone we asked was very helpful. Then there was Pam Simon's perfectionism. It meant no erasures. A copy of the key pages [title, contents, summary] were lodged with five minutes to spare, by Pam and myself - we ran several blocks to the old State Office Block. Pam found out that lodgement of these pages constituted meeting the deadline for submissions.

Only the very curious – and, given the times, brave - visited the WEL office. I was there the day Ian McPhee, then a Liberal Party MP, strolled in, sat on the corner of the desk and asked what our purpose was. Very polite, always. A few quite desperate women did find and venture into the office, in response to the proposed 1975 Family Law legislation. They shared their stories; many were quite tragic. One was a woman who'd lived in a mansion until her husband divorced her. He was able to make his income look miniscule for the purposes of the divorce hearing. She ended up with almost nothing, living in a back room of a former neighbour's mansion where she had once been entertained as a guest.

WEL members all thoroughly enjoyed the International Women's Day marches – most of us had never been in a public protest before. Eventually, thousands of women took part. On one such march, a man ran out of a hotel as the march passed in the midday sun. He rushed at the crowd of women, shouting *go home you bitches,* just as my row drew level with him. I was on the outside and expected to be hit by his huge fist. Then there were the memorable days bringing the newsletter together. The story is best told by Diana Wyndham.[76]

Pam asked me to take her place in the office while she devoted herself to organising the 1985 Mid-Decade UN Convention on Status of Women. Such was Pam's dedication and her role, it most likely would not have been the successful event it was, without her. I'd broken my right arm, but after Pam did a quick inspection, she saw that my fingers were free and assured me I would be able to use the electric typewriter. The event attracted attention and support from across the political and public spectrum. Women's organisations of all backgrounds were keen to get involved. On the day, as the Town Hall was filling, Helen Reddy's *I am Woman* filled the hall, and helped build the excitement. But not for everyone, and women from a conservative organisation ran around with their hands over their ears.

For over two decades, Pam was unrelenting in her commitment to WEL, and the fate of women who had previously been overlooked in the community. Even on a family holiday by the beach, Pam sat under the umbrella handwriting letters to every MP, advocating on behalf of WEL.

About the author:

Glenda Gartrell

Glenda has lived in Sydney for decades but always described herself as from the country where she was born, educated and had her first job. Significantly, it was where she met her partner of 60 years. They had three children; now, she has five grandchildren and five great-grandchildren.

Glenda moved to Sydney and joined the ferment of the 1970s revolution in women's lives. She continues membership of the Women's Electoral Lobby (WEL), the key driver of legislated change that directly affected women and some of their husbands. She has been a community activist ever since.

Her university degrees coincided with a busy household of six for most of her student period. She also had her own business.

One of the significant changes she helped introduce was getting a community representative into areas that were previously the private domain of management in both public

and private sector agencies, and this was when the senior managers were all male.

Before she took up paid employment, she was a community voice in various areas, including management of life-sentence prisoners, CSIRO animal ethics advice, public education advocacy, food standards in retail outlets and a federal government inquiry.

She also had a role in executive government [research & speech writer to NSW Premier], followed by a decade in NSW government departments before she launched her government relations consultancy.

After her husband died, Glenda joined a writing group and hasn't had a spare moment since.

olderwomensydney.org

Acknowledgements

I would not have begun this book without Judy Higgs, and I would never have completed it without her positive feedback, constant interest and encouragement.

David Hale has patiently listened, offered comment and advice and I am indebted to him for his input and encouragement.

Peter Thomas whose male perspective and thoughtful commentary prompted areas I had overlooked.

Throughout, Ellie Brasch's professional assistance and advice has kept me focused. I am thankful for all this but especially for urging me to tell my story.

I am indebted to my friends who generously shared the stories of their varied and interesting lives.

And to my family whose interest, love and support has never wavered.

Endnotes

1 - *Camper's widow breaks silence after split verdict*, The New Daily, 26/06/2024.

2 - Matters, Brain, *The power of social touch: How a loving caress really can ease anxiety.* Netherlands Institute for Neuroscience - KNAW. *New study highlights the benefit of touch on mental and physical health.* ScienceDaily, 8 April 2024. www.sciencedaily.com/releases/2024/04/240408130610.htm.

3 - Wilson, Sarah. *The anxiety – and danger – of isolation when you live alone. Sarahwilson.com*, April 9, 2020.

4 - Marquez, Gabriel Garcia, 1927-2014.

5 - Lister, Kat. The Observer, 14/05/23. *I miss the sex. Why are the sex lives of the bereaved still a taboo?*

6 - Bakan, Sezen, *Craving human touch? Scientists have worked out why hugs feel good, The New Daily*, 5/05/2022.

7 - *How To Cope with Loneliness and Isolation*, Griefline.org.au, 5/12/2021.

8 - Marson, Katrina, T*eaching kids that sex is shameful can harm them for life*. SMH, 31/01/23.

9 - Hunt, Elle, *Clitbait: 10 things you didn't know about the clitoris*, Guardian, 23/01/2017.

10 - Szoeke, Cassandra, Professor, *Secrets of Women's Healthy Ageing: Living Better, Living Longer*, 2021. Melbourne University Press.

11 - Law, Benjamin, Stephanie Alexander: *Food isn't intrinsically sexy, but it can certainly work up an atmosphere*. SMH, 10/09/21.

12 - Von Mohr, Kirsch, & Fotopoulou, *Lonely for Touch? A Narrative Review on the Role of Touch in Loneliness*, Cambridge University Press. 2022.

13 - Sima, Richard, *The power of social touch; How a loving caress really can ease anxiety*, George Wylesol for the Washington Post, 9/02/23.

14 - Berry, Sarah, *Sharing worries with a confidante can build shield against dementia: study*, SMH, 1/05/23.

15 - World Health Organisation, *The Principles of Pleasure*, Netflix, 1 March 2022.

16 - Australian Women's Weekly, first published in1933.https://www.womensweekly.com.au.

17 - McKay, Hugh, *Three Generations: The changing values and political outlook of Australians*. A paper presented in the Department of the Senate Occasional Lecture Series at Parliament House, August 1997. https://www.aph.gov.au. https://www.aph.gov.au, Papers on parliament No 31, June 1998 PDF 504KB.

18 - Summers, Anne, *The little pill that changed the world*, SMH 8/07/2010.

19 - https://en.wikipedia.org›wiki › Judeo-Christian ethics.

20 - Kenneth J Facer, Erratic society: Pill is blamed. SMH 25/05/1982.

21 - Wyndham, Diana, *Norman Haire and the Study of Sex,* Sydney University Press, 2012.

22 - Australian Women's Weekly [AWW], page 19, 17/09/1938.

23 - AWW, page 18, 9/07/1958.

24 - AWW, page 27, 9/07/1958.

25 - AWW page 4, 9/07/1958.

26 - Wyndham, Diana. Memoir of a *Late Blooming Feminist. Unpublished.*

27 - Women's Electoral Lobby https://www.wel.org.au.

28 - Wyndham, ibid.

29 - NSW Women's Coordination Unit, https://ednaryan.net.au›recipients › helen-lorange, Ziller, Alison, Equal Employment Opportunity, EEO Director, the University of Newcastle, Australia; Sobski, Jozefa, NSW Education Department, Social Development Unit, https://www.wel.org.au/wel_congratulates_jozefa_sobski_am.

30 - Hil, Richard, *Ageism very much alive in society,* SMH, 25/08/21. Krasovistsky, Marlene, *Why Kochie bristled at casual ageism,* SMH, 13/04/24.

31 - AWW, page 48, 15/05/1963.

32 - Jessop, Vicky, Secrets of the Female Orgasm on Channel 4 Review: a powerful look at a taboo topic, 1/09/2023. Standard.co.uk.

33 - Hunt, Elle, *Clitbait: 10 things you didn't know about the clitoris.* www.theguardian.com, 23/01/2017.

34 - Reid, Elizabeth, inaugural head of a women's advisory group to Prime Minister, Gough Whitlam. https://www.whitlam.org › publications › Elizabeth-Reid-legacy-paper.

35 - Older Women's Network, https://ownnsw.org.au.

36 - L'Orange, Helen, who pioneered the North Sydney community network known as the Hub; Eisenstein, H, (1996) *Inside Agitators- Australian Democrats and the State,* Allen &Unwin, Page 102. Curtis, Katina, Summers, Ann, *Violence or poverty: The dire choice faced by nearly half a million women.* SMH, 7 Jul 2022.

37 - Hartcher, Peter, *Good luck draining this swamp.* SMH, News Review, 10/08/24.

38 - Brown, Breve, *Shame,* 7.30 Report, Australian Broadcasting Commission, 2 Dec 2021.

39 - Liberal Party of Australia. A centre-right party. https://en.wikipedia.org.

40 - Gillard, Julia, Editor; *Not now, not ever,* Vintage Books, 2023. Significant point in the speech made to Australian Parliament, that *enough is enough,* and contributors who detail the way gender has underpinned inequality.

41 - Wade, Matt and Attia, Monica, *Diverse view from the top, Sun-Herald* 6/02/2022.

42 - Buttrose, Ita. https://www.abc.net.au›.

43 - Yasa, Dilvin, *Viva las 80s,* Sunday Life, Sun Herald, 14/07/2024.

44 - *Cougars, Grannies, Evil Stepmothers, and Menopausal Hot Flashers:* Roles, Representations of Age, and the Non-traditional Romance Heroine (Exegesis).

45 - Harold and Maude, 1971. https://www.imdb.com.

46 - Tuohy, Wendy, *Boobs too big! No wonder women don't go on TV,* SMH 14/03/23.

47 - Jones, Caroline. *ABC veteran reporter dies. https://www.news.com.au.* 20/05/2022.

48 - The *PBS News Hour*, SBS Channel 30. Due to licensing agreements and copyright restrictions, PBS content is geo-blocked, making it unavailable to viewers in Australia.

49 - Hornery, Andrew, *Pressure to look 'hot' is taking the joy out of getting older*. Sun-Herald, 28/05/23.

50 - Menadue, John. *Pearls & Irritations*, 31 July 2024. https://johnmenadue.com.

51 - Nile, Fred, former MLC, NSW Parliament.

52 - Harford, Tim. *The Tiny Pill which gave birth to an economic revolution*. 22/05/2017 bbc.com World Service

53 - AWW, Betty Kjelgaard, 1/09/1954.

54 - AWW, *Wolf at the door*, 9/07/1952.

55 - AWW, page 48, 15/05/1963.

56 - L'Orange, Helen, has demonstrated outstanding feminist leadership during her long careers in NSW and Commonwealth Government Departments, and in volunteering with the Women's Electoral Lobby (WEL).

57 - Lewin, Dr Evelyn, *The Middle Ages*. Sun-Herald Sunday life, 10/12/23.

58 - ibid.

59 - Ring Anne. *I'm old and happy about it, so don't dare call me young for my age*. SMH, 6/08/2021.

60 - Grandma style: *brands still ignoring women over size 14*, Sun-Herald 27/03/2022.

61 - Lewin, Dr Evelyn, ibid.

62 - Banwell, Ingrid, *Beware Invisible Angry Older Women: you won't see us coming*. SMH 9/1/2023.

63 - Krasovitsky, Marlene, *Why Kochie bristled at casual ageism*, SMH, 12/04/2022.

64 - Hurstans, Claire, *Ageist potshots hurt older people everywhere*. SMH, 20/02/24.

65 - Dating site for older women. oldersingle.com.au.

66 - eSafety Commissioner: Online safety. https://www.esafety.gov.au.

67 - Annual Report on STIs, UNSW Kirby Institute, 18/12/23 https://www.kirby.unsw.edu.au.

68 - Vidal, Gore. *The United States of Amnesia: Tribeca Review,* Frank Scheck, www.hollywoodreporter.com. 19/04/2013.

69 - Cohen, Lyndell, *We don't have any right to judge them. They never stop feeling*. The Garden Suburb Aged Care Facility Manager, Newcastle, NSW.

70 - *Second world war veteran, 100, ties knot in Normandy*. Guardian Weekly, 14/06/24.

71 - Baker, John, *I've stopped sleeping with my wife. Now we really sleep*. SMH 2/08/24.

72 - Hennezel, Marie de, *Sex after Sixty*, Scribe 2017.

73 - Darling, Gwenda. Ironmonger, Lauren, *Dealing with desires undiminished*. SMH 22/09/2024.

74 - ibid.

75 - ibid.

76 - ibid.